Vera Lex

Journal of the International Natural Law Society

New Series Volume 9, Numbers 1&2 Winter 2008

Pace University Press
1 Pace Plaza
New York, NY 10038

ISBN 978-0-944473-92-4

Contributors
Address all submissions and correspondence to The Editor, VERA LEX, Pace University, Department of Philosophy & Religious Studies, 1 Pace Plaza, New York, NY 10038. Please send two copies of the paper submitted. Include adequate margins, double space everything (text, notes, works cited, quotations). Use U.S. spelling and punctuation style, (e.g. periods inside quotation marks; "double quotes" for opening and closing quotations). The University of Chicago Manual of Style, 13th Edition, is to be consulted regarding matters of style. Notes are to be numbered consecutively (in Arabic numerals) and placed at the bottom of the page.

Subscribers
VERA LEX is published annually by Pace University Press, 41 Park Row, Room 1510, New York, NY 10038. Subscription price: $40. Please send all subscription inquiries to: PaceUP@pace.edu

Indexing and Abstracting
VERA LEX is indexed in Philosopher's Index.

VERA LEX, the journal of the International Natural Law Society, was established to communicate and dialogue on the subject of natural law and natural right, to introduce natural law philosophy into the mainstream of contemporary thought, and to strengthen the current revived interest in the discussion of morals and law and advance its historical research.

Why do we use a shell (*Nautilus pomplilus Linnaeus*) to symbolize vera lex? The logarithmic spiraling and overlapping chambers of the shell are endless. They suggest a patterned development and evolution that, by its radial and circular design, never comes to an end. This means that the shell is at once specific and real, while its form, like law, is abstract and ideal.

The pattern of a shell is, like good law, uniform, regular and reliable. It can therefore be anticipated and known. The pattern of a shell is balanced, like justice. Una iustitia.

A shell is a biological being. Like law, it has life and dynamic. It grows. (There is an average of thirty growth lines per chamber, one for every day in the lunar cycle, suggesting that a new chamber is put down each lunar month and a new growth line each day, thus recording two different natural rhythms, lunar and solar.)

The shell is a universal and common object known to everyone. A shell is not soft tissue easily destroyed. And yet, like liberty, it is fragile in certain respects if stepped on with an iron boot. It has to be guarded with vigilance or it is crushed.

In every shell lives a nautilus. If the shell is law, the nautilus (snail) is a person—it is alive—person and law. Their destinies, like person and law, are interdependent.

Vera Lex

leges innumerae, una iustitia

CONTENTS

NEW SERIES VOLUME 9, NUMBERS 1 & 2 — WINTER 2008

EDITORIAL

This issue is dedicated to Professor Virginia Black in appreciation for her legacy to natural law scholarship. Prof. Black founded the International Natural Law Society in 1979 and the first "newsletter," that later would become *Vera Lex*, was published in 1980. Until her retirement in 2000, Virginia's tireless efforts to revitalize natural law have been partially responsible for its remarkable resurgence. Prof. Black, in her initial goodbye (she was encouraged to stay on in 1995 for another five years) wrote, "Since the first issue of *Vera Lex* in 1980, I have labored to refresh the ancient insights and to bring new life into this great enterprise. With the technical, financial, and intellectual support of loyal associates at Pace, of scholars and thinkers everywhere, and with the help of my husband and children, *Vera Lex* is now a living entity in many law schools and private libraries. For this I am deeply grateful."

These sentiments are appropriate again today with *Vera Lex*'s uncertain future. This is the last volume of *Vera Lex* I will edit, and possibly the final issue unless someone assumes the editorship. These last eight years as editor have been an ongoing challenge to continue the level of excellence established by Prof. Black. Whether I have been successful the reader will have to decide. We did cover some new territory by introducing natural law to environmental issues, globalization (neoliberalism), feminism, and Asian thought. Also, we gave *Vera Lex* a new look and the bulk of the administrative responsibilities were taken over by Pace University Press, to whom I owe much gratitude; thank you, Professor Mark Hussey.

Over the years as editor, Professor Black produced a large volume of essays and editorials, which made the choice of what to include a bit daunting. In the end we chose those works that represent the broad scope of Prof. Black's interests. It is refreshing to hear Virginia's voice once again in these final days of *Vera Lex*. Maybe they will inspire someone to continue the conversation.

RLC

NYC 2008

FEATURED ARTICLES

AQUINAS AND MACINTYRE ON NATURAL LAW: METAPHYSICS AND PRACTICE[1]

David Lorenzo

The aim of this paper is to analyze the concept and the basis of natural law in Aquinas and Alasdair MacIntyre in order to show that those two treatments are different from each other but complementary in ways to recover and to define natural law. It can be useful also to find the connections between Aquinas and MacIntyre.[2] For my argument, I'm going to use the *Summa Theologica* by Aquinas, and the works written by MacIntyre from 1981, when he published his famous book *After Virtue*.[3]

My argument is divided in three parts. The first is about the concept and the foundation of natural law in Aquinas; the second, about the concept and the foundation of natural law in MacIntyre. The third part, as a conclusion, is an exposition of the complementary points of the authors' ideas.

AQUINAS: THE METAPHYSICAL FOUNDATION OF NATURAL LAW

In this part, we are going to look briefly at the way followed by Aquinas to define and to state the main features of natural law. We can clearly call this way the *metaphysical way*. Aquinas starts from

[1] This paper comes from a lecture delivered at the international conference "Rediscovering the Roots and the Common Values of Western Culture: the Concept of Law in Thomas Aquinas" (Palermo, Italy, October 25-30, 2005), a conference organized in the frame of Project Culture 2000 ("Saint Thomas Education Project"), financed by the European Union. The Italian translation of this paper is going to be published under the title "Tommaso d'Aquino e MacIntyre sulla legge naturale : metafisica e pratica" (in Di Blasi ed., *Riscoprire le radici e i valori comuni della civilta occidentale*, proceedings of the conference).

[2] There are currently many authors and theories in the whole contemporary debate on natural law, but here the author only wants to pay attention to some general aspects starting from MacIntyre's thought.

[3] Although his thought has changed from this year after and he keeps thinking and writing on different issues.

Metaphysics, Psychology and Anthropology to define natural law. Let's analyze this path.

1.1 The soul and its powers

According to Aquinas, rational soul is the form of human being.[4] Aristotle says in *De Anima* that soul is the essence of living beings, and soul, in human beings, is the principle of movement and thought. Because of this, the proper nature of human being is a rational nature, which makes a being *human*. The ultimate source of human operations is that nature, for "the nature of a thing is the first in everything".[5] Nature is the own being of something.[6] The substantial form, then, is the first principle of action, but not the proximate principle—says Aquinas.[7]

The proximate principles of action in human being are the powers.[8] Soul provides human being with some powers, although those powers are different from the very essence of the soul, for the powers don't belong to the essence of the substance.[9] Nevertheless, they are *natural properties* of the soul, special accidents.[10] The soul, as mere form, is an act not ordained to a further act. The soul is first act and only through its powers the soul is ordained to a further act, which is the second act.[11]

Then the soul is one and the powers are many. Aquinas says that a number of things which proceed from one thing must proceed in a certain order. So there is an order among the powers of the soul.[12] And this order is also in the objects and in the acts perfomed by those powers.[13]

[4] Aquinas, *Summa Theologica* (NY: Benziger Brothers, 1947), I-II, q. a. 3; I-II, q. 91, a. 6. All Aquinas' references belong to the *Summa Theologica*. We indicate only the part of the *Summa* (with roman numerals), the question and the article.

[5] Aquinas, I, q. 82,a. 1.

[6] Aquinas, I, q. 80,a. 1.

[7] Aquinas, I, q. 77, a. 1.

[8] Aquinas, I, q. 78, a. 4.

[9] Aquinas, I, q. 77, a. 1.

[10] Aquinas, I, q. 77, a. 1.

[11] Aquinas, I, q. 77, a. 1.

[12] Aquinas, I, q. 77, a. 4.

[13] Aquinas, I, q. 77, a. 4, ad 2.

In living beings, this order depends on the differents souls: vegetative soul, sensitive soul and rational soul. In them, there is a degree of dependence in respect with the need for corporeal organs and qualities. Rational soul's operation exceeds corporeal nature and is not perfomed by any corporeal organ.[14] That's why Aquinas says that the subject of will and understanding is the soul, for these operations are performed without corporeal organ. The subject of sensitive and vegetative operations is the composite soul-body, since they perform their operations by means of the body.[15] The vegetative and sensitive powers are not natural properties of the soul alone but of the composite.[16]

All the powers belong to the soul as their principle, not as their subject, for the composite has the powers to perform its operations thanks to the soul.[17] The composite is actualized by the soul. The accidental form is caused by a substantial form according to the proper potentiality of the accidental form. Because of this, the powers of the soul flow from the essence of the soul.[18]

The next step in our explanation is the relation between the power and its object. Aquinas tells us that a power is defined by its proper act (to which it's directed), and this by its object.[19] Therefore, there is an essential relation between a power and its *proper* object. Because of this, Aquinas says that the object of the operations must have some relation to the soul. And this relation happens in a twofold manner:

a) the object has a natural aptitude to be united to the soul and to be in it by its likeness.

b) the soul itself has a natural inclination or tendency to something extrinsic.[20]

[14] Aquinas, I, q. 78, a. 1.

[15] Aquinas, I, q. 77, a. 5. The subject of the power is the subject of its operation, for the subject of an operative power is that which is able to operate, and every accident denominates its own subject (I, q. 77 , a. 5).

[16] Aquinas, I, q. 77, a. 8, ad 2. Aquinas argues this idea against the objection that all the powers remain in soul after death because they are properties of the soul (I, q. 77,a. 8,ad 2).

[17] Aquinas, I, q. 77, a. 5, ad 1.

[18] Aquinas, I, q. 77, a. 6.

[19] Aquinas, I, q. 77, a. 3.

[20] Aquinas, I, q. 78, a. 1.

1.2 Essence, law and inclination

An inclination is such in respect with an essence. Aquinas says that every inclination results from a form.[21] for every form is inclined to something. An inclination follows every form: this is what Aquinas calls a *natural inclination, natural appetite* (*appetitus naturalis*).[22] Then this natural appetite proceeds from the form existing in a thing.[23]

Every being has, by its own nature, the inclination to something,[24] which is something suitable, that's to say: which is its proper good.[25] It has to be said that, for Aquinas, something *natural* is something proper or corresponding to a being according to its specific nature[26] and the unnatural is that opposed to it.[27]

We have already mentioned that the soul is one and the powers are many.[28] Because of this, every power tends to a different object, but a nature, as first and single principle of action, tends only to one thing.[29] In every *genus*, as it implies a common form for the things included in that *genus*, there must be a commond end, a last end of the *genus*, an end shared by all the members of this *genus*.[30] *The last end or the united tendency of a being consists in the fulfilment of the perfection of this being.*[31]

In the light of what we have said so far, we can now understand that, according to Aquinas, there are some things desired naturally by human will: the good in general (to which the will tends like every power tends to its object), the last end, and, in general, that which is suitable to man

[21] Aquinas, I-II, q. 8, a. 1.

[22] Aquinas, I, q. 80, a. 1.

[23] Aquinas, I-II, q. 8, a. 1.

[24] Aquinas, I, q. 78, a. 1, ad 3.

[25] Aquinas, I-II, q. 8, a. 1. The good is that which has the nature of an end (I-II, q. 1,a. 4). Aquinas says that the suitableness is a relation. The consideration of something as good depends, then, on the conditions of two elements: the object and the subject (I-II, q. 9, a. 2). Moreover, there are two senses of *good*: the good common to every being (*bonum commune*); and the good for a concrete nature (I-II, q. 54, a. 3, ad 2).

[26] Aquinas, I-II, q. 51, a. 1.

[27] Aquinas, I-II, q. 6, a. 5. Another meaning of *natural* is also that proper to an individual nature (I-II, q. 51, a. 1). More meanings of *nature* (I-II, q. 10, a. 1).

[28] Aquinas, I, q. 77, a. 4.

[29] Aquinas, I-II, q. 1, a. 5; q. 1, a. 7, ad 3.

[30] Aquinas, I-II, q. 1, a. 5.

[31] Aquinas, I-II, q. 1, a. 7.

according to his nature (the goods of the other powers, like the truth; or to be, to live, and goods related to the human existence).[32] *Since being precedes to the will,*[33] *there are things desired by man before and independently of the proper act of the will.*[34]

It can be said that the concept of inclination connects Metaphysics and Psychology with natural law and practical reason. "Law is a rule and measure of acts, whereby man is induced to act or is restrained from acting."[35] Let's remember the definition of law given by Aquinas: "an ordinance of reason for the common good, made by him who has care of the community, and promulgated."[36]

According to Aquinas, natural law has been promulgated by God by instilling it into human being.[37] Everything participates in the eternal law because, for this law, every being tends to its proper acts and objects. In the rational being, this participation is called *natural law*[38], *whose aim is to distinguish evil and good.*[39]

As we have seen above, human essence and its proper powers imply some natural inclinations. The precepts of natural law and their internal order are based on those human natural inclinations.

1st) Human being, as a being, shares with the rest of beings the tendency to keep its existence. So everything related to keep life and to avoid its destruction belongs to natural law.

2nd) Human being, as an animal, shares with the rest of animals the tendency to some proper goods, like reproduction and children's education.

3rd) Finally, human being has some proper inclinations as a human being, like the inclination to truth about God, to live in community, etc.[40] Those inclinations show or indicate the goods for human being. In this sense, we can say that they give the first content to the first principle of practical reason: good has to be done and evil has to be

[32] Aquinas, I-II, q. 10, a. 1.
[33] Aquinas, I-II, q. 10, a. 1, ad 1.
[34] Aquinas, I-II, q. 10, a. 1,ad 1.
[35] Aquinas, I-II, q. 90, a. 1.
[36] Aquinas, I-II, q. 90, a. 4.
[37] Aquinas, I-II, q. 90, a. 4, ad 1.
[38] Aquinas, I-II, q. 91, a. 2.
[39] Aquinas, I-II, q. 91, a. 2.
[40] Aquinas, I-II, q. 94, a. 2.

avoided. The precepts of natural law come from those inclinations and their order.[41] They are the first or common principles of practical reason, which are the premises for the secondary principles.[42] Reason cannot fail to know the first principles of natural law, but it can fail to know or define the secondary principles and also when it judges about particular cases.[43]

According to what we have said so far, it can be said that, in a certain sense, the very inclinations of the human being have a certain character of law. Aquinas says that law exists in the measuring principle in an essential way, and in the thing measured in a participate way: every inclination of something regulated by law can be considered law by participation.[44] Since the human form is the rational soul and every being tends to act according to its form, to act according to reason is the proper inclination of human being.[45] In this participate way, the rule and measure of human acts is the reason.[46] In fact, for human being, to be virtuous is precisely to act according to reason.[47]

MACINTYRE: THE PRACTICAL FOUNDATION OF NATURAL LAW

Natural law is a topic which MacIntyre has introduced in his thought recently. MacIntyre is not a metaphysician, although a metaphysical scheme is implicit in his thought. His arguments start usually from practical fields. In fact, one of the most important concepts in his thought is the concept of *practice*. MacIntyre talks about natural law from the practices. Practices are the proper field or way to know and to think about natural law. That's why we call this way the *practical way*.[48]

[41] Aquinas, I-II, q. 94, a. 2.
[42] Aquinas, I-II, q. 91, a. 3.
[43] Aquinas, I-II, q. 99, a. 2, ad 2.
[44] Aquinas, I-II, q. 91, a. 6.
[45] Aquinas, I-II, q. 94, a. 3; I-II, q. 91, a. 6.
[46] Aquinas, I-II, q. 90, a. 1. Because of this, Aquinas says that human reason is not in itself the rule and measure of the things, but the principles grasped by it work as general rules for human actions (I-II, q. 91, a. 3, ad 2).
[47] Aquinas, I-II, q. 94, a. 3.
[48] Before starting my explanation, I'd like to mention that my paper shows a synthetic view

2.1 Human being and practices

For MacIntyre, the practice is very important because the development of human being (his powers) take place only in it, as we can read in the paper "Plain Persons and Moral Philosophy: Rules, Virtues and Goods."[49] In his book *After Virtue*, the author defines the practice as "any coherent and complex form of socially established cooperative human activity through which goods internal to that form of activity are realized in the course of trying to achieve those standards of excellence which are appropriate to, and partially definitive of, that form of activity, with the result that human powers to achieve excellence, and human conceptions of the ends and goods involved, are systematically extended."[50] Sciences, architecture, farming are examples of practices.[51] Therefore: a practice is an activity with some internal goods with some standards of excellence. Academic life of any university can be considered, for instance, a practice; and somehow this conference is a practice or at least part of the practice which is the academic life of this university.

The elements of a practice according to MacIntyre are three: goods, models of excellence (or authorities), and rules. Let's consider briefly each one of them. Regarding the goods, the author distinguishes two kinds of them: external goods and internal goods. The internal ones are those goods referred to the proper excellence of a concrete practice. The best building and the best way to design it are internal goods to the architecture. Moreover, the external ones

---

of the issue; I mean: what I'm going to explain as a unity is not explained in the same way by MacIntyre. The author talks about a concrete issue in several points of his books and papers and in different ways. He usually doesn't explain one issue systematically, but in several points and moments. That's why it's necessary to try to summarize or synthesize his ideas.

[49] MacIntyre, "Plain Persons and Moral Philosophy: Rules, Virtues and Goods" (Thomas Aquinas Lecture, 1991 in Univ. of Dallas), *American Catholic Philosophical Quarterly* 66, no. 1 (Winter 1992), 3-20. Reprinted (with little changes) in *The MacIntyre Reader*, ed. Kelvin Knight (Cambridge: Polity Press, 1998), 139. We use this last edition.

[50] Alasdair MacIntyre, *After Virtue: A Study in Moral Theory* (London: Duckworth, 1981; and: Notre Dame: University of Notre Dame Press, 1981). Revised version: *After Virtue: A Study in Moral Theory* (Notre Dame: University of Notre Dame Press, 1984), 187-188. We indicate the pages of the last edition.

[51] MacIntyre, *After Virtue*, 187-188, 200-201.

are those goods not related directly to the proper excellence of a practice. These kinds of goods can be achieved through many kinds of practices and can be independent of the achivement of the internal goods to the practice. These goods are money, power, prestige and so on. Therefore, internal goods are the proper or essential *telos* of a practice.[52]

Rules are necessary elements of a practice because they are the guidelines or the norms to be followed by the individual if he wants to achieve the internal goods to the practices.[53] Some rules have to be observed because they take the individual to the excellence in a practice. It's necessary for us, for instance, to train weekly if we want to make a good football team

The third element of practices are models or authorities. According to MacIntyre, they are necessary because the individual needs to know the rules and the goods of the practices, and he also has to learn to apply the rules and to realize the internal good. The individuals need some people to learn and to practice these elements: they are the models or authorities.[54]

Finally, we can mention that virtues are the qualities through which the individual can distinguish and realize the internal goods to the practice, and follow the models and the rules related to it. According to MacIntyre, there are some virtues without which the individual cannot achieve the internal goods to the practice: justice, prudence, etc.[55]

[52] MacIntyre, *After Virtue*, 188-194; *Three Rival Versions of Moral Enquiry: Encyclopaedia, Genealogy, and Tradition*, The Gifford lectures delivered in 1988 in Univ. of Edimburg (Notre Dame: ND Press, 1990), 64-65.

[53] A. MacIntyre, *After Virtue*, 194-195; *Whose Justice? Which Rationality?* (Notre Dame: University of Notre Dame Press, 1988), 31-32.

[54] MacIntyre, *After Virtue*, 194-195.

[55] MacIntyre, *After Virtue*, 195-196; "Nietzsche O Aristotele?," in *Conversazioni Americane*, ed. Giovanna Borradori (Roma-Bari: Editori Laterza, 1994), 169-187. English transl.: "Nietzsche or Aristotle?", in *The American Philosopher: Conversations with Quine, Davidson, Putnam, Nozick, Danto, Rorty, Cavell, MacIntyre, and Kuhn* (Chicago: University of Chicago Press, 1994), 137-152. Reprinted with the title: "An Interview with Giovanna Borradori" in *The MacIntyre Reader*, ed. Kelvin Knight (Cambridge: Polity Press, 1998), 262. We use this last edition.

So far we have talked about the main elements of a practice (goods, rules and authorities). For MacIntyre, practices are the natural field or place where individuals act and live. Social and individual life are structured by practices, which take place in some institutions and in a concrete history or tradition. Every practice is part of a history and a tradition. An individual life is composed of many practices: someone can act as a father, as a lawyer, as a member of different associations and so on.

However, MacIntyre, in *After Virtue*, realizes, of course, that there are practices which are evil in themselves: for instance, torture, sadomasochistic sexuality, etc.[56] If every practice has its internal good, how is it possible to consider evil or wrong a practice in itself? The author answers that we need an external good to the practices to judge about this. This external good is what MacIntyre calls *flourishing* in his book *Dependent Rational Animals*. The *flourishing* is the development of the powers that human being possesses as a human being, or, in other words, how should human being live.[57] At this point, we should ask ourselves which is the relation between these three concepts we are talking about: *practice*, *flourishing* and *natural law*. This is the purpose of the next part of this paper.

2.2 Practice and natural law

According to what we have said so far, MacIntyre says that an individual has to be able to make two distinctions:

1) Regarding the internal good to the practice, he has to distinguish between what seems good for him at this moment and what is really good according to the practice.

2) Regarding the flourishing, he has to distinguish what is good for him now and here and what is good in itself, for everybody.[58]

Therefore, the final good beyond the goods of the practices is necessary to judge the same practices. Besides this, a final good is necessary to explain the human existence, that's to say: there are

[56] MacIntyre, *After Virtue*, 200.

[57] MacIntyre, *Dependent Rational Animals: Why Human Beings Need the Virtues* (London: Duckworth, 1999), 63-65, 76-77.

[58] MacIntyre, *Three Rival Versions of Moral* Enquiry, 126-127; "Plain Persons and Moral Philosophy: Rules, Virtues and Goods", 140.

many practices in which an individual can be involved but the individual itself is unity, one and the same person in those different practices. The existence of a final good related to the individual as a whole, as a unity, is necessary.

Because of this, MacIntyre distinguishes three meanings of the concept of *good*:

1) *Good* as a means to another good, which is a good in itself.

2) *Good* according to a concrete practice. In this sense, an individual is good as a father, as a teacher and so on.[59]

3) *Good* as a human being, as a member of the human species. In this sense, an individual is good if he is flourishing as such.[60] In fact, this third sense of the concept is the main one for MacIntyre: something is good for an individual if it contributes to his flourishing.[61] Therefore, flourishing is the final good, the final *telos* of human life.

For MacIntyre, a judgement on human flourishing is a judgment about whether an individual has developed his human faculties. Because of this, he says that his concept of good is *functional*. It's a factual statement: it's a judgment on the fact of the flourishing itself, rather than a subjective judgment. The author argues that we cannot define what a watch is without the idea of a *good watch*, which implies a concrete function. So just as we cannot define *watch* without the concept of *good watch*, it's impossible to define what a human being is without the idea of a *good human being*, that's to say, without the idea of flourishing, which is his proper function.[62] Let's remember that, for Aristotle, human nature is not only an essence but also an end, the *telos* of human being.[63]

'What is the content of that flourishing?', we can ask ourselves. MacIntyre answers that an individual has flourished when he is able to define adequately the good and when he has reached a certain degree of virtues. Virtues are necessary to

[59] MacIntyre, *Dependent Rational Animals*, 65-66.

[60] MacIntyre, *Dependent Rational Animals*, 66.

[61] MacIntyre, *Whose Justice? Which Rationality?*, 110-111. I would like to thank Dr. MacIntyre for a personal conversation on this issue (September 2004).

[62] MacIntyre, *After Virtue*, 157-161. Fuller calls this scheme the *form-function-virtue scheme*. Michael Fuller, *Making Sense of MacIntyre* (Aldershot: Ashgate, 1998), 5.

[63] Aristotle, *Politics* 1252b8-9.

define and to realize the good.[64] That's why the author says, in fact, that flourishing is rather "the kind of life which it is the best for human beings to live."[65]

The relation between flourishing—the final end—and natural law is that the precepts or norms of natural law are the guides for human being to the final good, to that flourishing. MacIntyre says that these norms, in their negative form, are like limits to the kind of lives where that human *telos* can be fulfilled.[66] "Those rules enjoin and prohibit certain types of action as such. It is only insofar as our actions conform to what those precepts require, and do so just because those precepts require it, that we can become the kind of people who are able to achieve that final good towards which we are directed by our nature. So the human good can be achieved only through a form of life in which the positive and negative precepts of the natural law are the norms governing our relationships."[67]

According to MacIntyre, human nature develops or flourishes following certain laws, laws which lead an individual to what he shares with other individuals.[68] And the basis of this inclination or tendency is the common human nature, the only true foundation for natural law.[69] If a rational nature tends to its development

[64] MacIntyre, *Dependent Rational Animals*, 158-159.

[65] We think that, for MacIntyre (although he doesn't use these words), finally the good is essentially what perfects or improves a nature (the author doesn't talk about the *bonum commune*) (like for Aquinas: I-II, q. 54, a. 3, ad 2), and, therefore, that towards/to what this nature tends (Aquinas, I-II, q. 1, a. 4; Aristotle, *Metaphysics* 1.983a32; *Nichomachean Ethics* 1.1094a2-3; 10.1173a1).

[66] MacIntyre, *Three Rival Versions of Moral Enquiry*, 139; "Plain Persons and Moral Philosophy: Rules, Virtues and Goods", 143; *Dependent Rational Animals*, ix-x. As an example of how important for a moral theory is this final good, we can look at the Ethics presented by Rawls in his book *A Theory of Justice*, where he says that there is no a final end for human being. Rawls, John, *A Theory of Justice* (Cambridge-Massachusetts, Belknap Press of Harvard University Press: 1978, 9th edition; 1st ed. 1971), 554.

[67] MacIntyre, "How Can We Learn What *Veritatis Splendor* Has To Teach?," *The Thomist* 58 (1994), 173.

[68] MacIntyre, "Wahre Selbsterkenntnis durch Verstehen unserer selbst aus der Perspektive anderer" (interview with Dmitri Nikulin)," *Deutsche Zeitschrift für Philosophie* 44, no. 4 (1996), 676-677.

[69] MacIntyre, "Theories of Natural Law in the Culture of Advanced Modernity," in *Common Truths: New Perspectives on Natural Law*, en Edward B. McLean (Wilmington, Delaware: ISI Books, 2000), 113.

according to proper features, it has to follow the law which guides this development: thus MacIntyre explains the necessary relation between *to be* and *ought to be.*[70] *That's why such a rules are not an external element to human life but rather an essential element of the best life possible for human beings, which is the aim of the rules.*[71] *Because of this, natural law is independent of civil laws but, at the same time, it has to inform them as well as the individual practical reasoning, for natural law is something previous to human knowledge and liberty, just as the same tendency to flourishing.*[72]

As we can see, MacIntyre—following Aquinas—thinks that common human nature is the only foundation for natural law and that this law implies and is directed to the final telos of human being.[73] However, the author thinks that the most difficult thing in the reflection on natural law is perhaps how to know and to define the precepts of that natural law.[74]

MacIntyre doesn't pay attention to the different levels or degrees of the precepts of natural law and, in fact, he doesn't offer a concrete definition of the concept of *natural law*, but the important idea here is that he thinks that the practices are the most important element in knowing and in defining them. That's why we are talking about the practices and the practical way.

For the author, natural law can be known and defined only from social practices, that's to say, from those activities in which the individual participates and which take place in a community.[75] In his paper "Natural Law Reconsidered" (of

[70] MacIntyre, "Plain Persons and Moral Philosophy: Rules, Virtues and Goods", 138-139; "Wahre Selbsterkenntnis durch Verstehen unserer selbst aus der Perspektive anderer (interview with Dmitri Nikulin)", 676-677.

[71] MacIntyre, "The Privatization of Good. An Inaugural Lecture," *The Review of Politics* 52, no. 3 (Summer 1990), 344.

[72] MacIntyre, "Plain Persons and Moral Philosophy: Rules, Virtues and Goods", 138-139; "Theories of Natural Law in the Culture of Advanced Modernity", 99.

[73] MacIntyre, *Three Rival Versions of Moral Enquiry*, 133-134.

[74] MacIntyre, "Natural Law Reconsidered (review of *Aquinas's Theory of Natural Law: An Analytic Reconstruction* by Anthony J. Lisska)," *International Philosophical Quarterly* 37, no. 1, issue 145 (March 1997), 98; "Theories of Natural Law in the Culture of Advanced Modernity,"95.

[75] MacIntyre, "Community, Law, and the Idiom and Rhetoric of Rights," *Listening: Journal of Religion and Culture* 26, no. 2 (1991), 110; "Theories of Natural Law in the Culture of Advanced Modernity," 109-110; "The *Theses on Feuerbach*: A Road Not Taken," in

1997), MacIntyre agrees with Aquinas in deriving natural law from inclinations of human nature.[76] Nevertheless, he prefers another way to natural law.[77]

MacIntyre tells us that, for Aquinas, an essential feature of any precept which is a law is that it is a rule of reason directed to common good. MacIntyre derives from this idea that, in order to define the good—and the goods—and the rules, the very inclinations of human nature aren't enough. Perhaps it's better to start with actions, debates and discussions about goods and rules which happen in practices when people are concerned about any common good.[78] Reflection and enquiry come after this fact, the *fact of the practice*, and then goods and rules necessary for everybody are found by people involved in these practices.[79]

In fact, MacIntyre thinks that this argument was proposed implicitly by Aquinas, for plain people at first don't derive natural law from metaphysical premises.[80] If human nature is known through its operations and through the actions realized by an individual, the practices are really important because they are the field or the context of those actions.[81] That's why the author concludes: "the recognition of natural law is a matter of how such practices are structured."[82]

As an example of this argument, we can look at what MacIntyre calls *ethics of enquiry*, which is involved in the practice of the moral and political debate or dialogue. The author defines it as "an additional authority that is independent of moral standpoint,"[83] and

Artifacts, Representations and Social Practice, eds. Carol C. Gould and Robert S. Cohen (Dordrecht: Kluwer, 1994), 277-290. Reprinted (with little changes) in *The MacIntyre Reader*, ed. Kelvin Knight (Cambridge: Polity Press, 1998), 234; we use this last edition; "Natural Law As Subversive: The Case of Aquinas," *Journal of Medieval and Early Modern Studies* 26, no. 1 (Winter 1996), 80-81.

[76] MacIntyre, "Natural Law Reconsidered," 98-99.

[77] I would like to thank Dr. MacIntyre for a personal conversation about this issue (August 2004).

[78] MacIntyre, "Natural Law Reconsidered," 98-99.

[79] MacIntyre, "Después de *Tras la virtud* (interview R. Yepes)," *Atlántida* 1, no. 4 (1990), 94-95.

[80] MacIntyre, "Natural Law Reconsidered," 98.

[81] MacIntyre, "Natural Law As Subversive: The Case of Aquinas," 80-81; "Theories of Natural Law in the Culture of Advanced Modernity," 94-95, 109-110.

[82] MacIntyre, "Natural Law As Subversive: The Case of Aquinas," 80-81.

[83] MacIntyre, "Moral Pluralism Without Moral Relativism," in *Proceedings of the Twentieth World Congress of Philosophy* 1, ed. K. Brinkmann (Philosophy Documentation Center, 1999), 6-7.

it's part of natural law. The liberty to express an opinion, the respect for people participating in the debate and so on: all of them are principles or virtues which form that *ethics of enquiry*. MacIntyre says that a true dialogue, a proper human dialogue, implies the acceptance of the ethics of enquiry. Perhaps someone doesn't define or state explicitly these rules but he is implicitly accepting them when he joins a public debate on moral or political issues.[84]

Certainly, there are other important points related to this issue to talk about, but we have already explained the main ideas of this paper. It's time to conclude by indicating how the *metaphysical way* and the *practical way* are complementary ways.

CONCLUSION: ESSENCE, PRACTICE AND NATURAL LAW

Why are the metaphysical way and the practical one complementary paths to state and to define natural law? This is the question we have to answer at this point.

1) The first conclusion is that one of the proper inclinations in human being includes the idea of practice. If to live in community is a natural inclination for human being, this inclination implies the idea of practice, for communities are articulated in practices.

2) The Thomistic principle that "operatio sequitur esse" (action follows being) implies personal relations (in respect with human being). Human actions are not just abstract facts but acts which take place within concrete relations and circumstances: in a community and family, in a concrete history and tradition, etc. These circumstances exist in practices.

3) The formal end of the law is the common good, referred both to the Universe's good in general and to the human being's good in particular. This common good implies social relations, that's to say practices, because common good is known or defined by individuals in practical relations where different concrete goods are known, achieved and are the object of reflection and debate. Goods and language and

[84] MacIntyre, "Moral Pluralism Without Moral Relativism," 7.

arguments to talk about them are learnt by human beings only in a communitarian context

.4) In relation to the former conclusion, we can say that the goods towards which human being is directed by his natural inclinations are determined and come out through the internal goods to the practices.

5) The inclination to virtue is a proper human inclination. Virtue is developed through acts, which need a communitarian structure, for human actions take place in practices and practices are the context where an individual receives the necessary help to develop his virtues (through models or authorities, for instance).

6) The explicit formulation or reflection about the first principles of natural law, and the improvement in deriving and formulating the secondary principles (and their implications) are all of them possible only through concrete practices. In respect with the secondary principles and judgments about particular cases, Aquinas says that an individual can fail to know them because of bad habits, which are developed in practices. So social practices can make it easier or harder for the individual to know and to follow natural law.

7) Human laws can be derived from natural law by conclusion or by determination. In both cases, the very fact of deriving them is possible and depends on the practices, not only because human laws regulate practices but also because the internal rules of the practices are related to human law and to natural law, at least implicitly.

To finish, let me say that the ways to natural law we have analyzed and related to each other are complementary ways so that the difference between them depends only on which point is stressed by each one. We can conclude, therefore, by saying that *practice* and *natural law* are concepts narrowly related to each other.

This statement can be useful in the complicated current situation of contemporary debate in philosophy because it makes it easier for metaphysics to enter some contemporary debates and, moreover, because people who don't accept or don't know any metaphysical schemes can start approaching natural law, at least in a certain degree.

NATURAL LAW IN LATE SCHOLASTIC HISPANIC THOUGHT, THE BRITISH COUNTER-EXAMPLE, AND THE PRATICAL CONSEQUENCES

William Pencak

I love the University of Salamancha; for when the Spaniards were in doubt as to the lawfulness of their conquering America, the University of Salamancha gave it as their opinion it was not lawful
Dr. Samuel Johnson[1]

Whatever virtues and defects may be found in the thought of the late Leo Strauss, we ought to be grateful for his distinction between natural law and natural right. Natural law emphasizes that there is an objective moral order in the world that societies and individuals violate at their peril, requiring mutual obligations of rulers and ruled, human beings and nature, and peoples and their deities (and those who represent them). Natural right stresses the ability of people to enjoy with limited restraints a variety of freedoms, including the right to obtain and possess property. Natural law is associated with the medieval tradition of philosophy that flowered in Spain in early modern times, natural right with the British empirical tradition of Locke and Hobbes whose rise accompanied that of the Anglo-Saxon nations in the modern world.[2] From each flowed a series of consequences as to how to treat conquered peoples and lands, which is the subject of this paper.

In "Hispanic Philosophy: Its Beginning and Golden Age," Jorge Gracia provides a list of neglected sixteenth-century thinkers who shaped the "thought of the world created by the European discovery of America."[3]The list is cited by John Deely in *New Beginnings: Early Modern Philosophy and Postmodern Thought,* a book literally dedicated, not to one or more persons as is customary, but "to the recovery of the Iberian intellectual culture of the Late Latin

[1] Leo Strauss, *Natural Right and History* (Chicago: University of Chicago Press, 1953).
[2] Jorge Gracia, "Hispanic Philosophy: Its Beginning and Golden Age," *The Review of Metaphysics* 46 (1993): 487-488.
[3] John Deely, *New Beginnings: Early Modem Philosophy and Postmodem Thought* (Toronto: University of Toronto Press, 1994), v, 33, 42.

Age," "a vein of pure philosophical gold which has only begun to be mined as the prejudices of contemporary scholarship in Anglo-American and Continental philosophy have begun to crumble in the face of historical facts at first grudgingly, now with increasing exuberance, brought to light in the academy."[4]

Now in Gracia's and Deely's list are two figures who may be neglected by philosophers, but who are well-known in the history of Latin America as pioneers in the development of notions of human rights: Vasco de Quiroga (1487?-1568) and, far more importantly, Bartolomé de Las Casas (1484-1566). My essay attempts three tasks. First, I will situate Quiroga and Las Casas as philosophers in the tradition which culminated with John Poinsot (1589-1644) and included Cajetan (1468-1534), Francisco de Vitoria (1492/3-1546), and Francisco Suarez (1548-1617). Second, as Deely has noted, their philosophy mattered: "intellectual foundations were laid in the world of the Iberian peninsula for the development of international law and for dealing with the general problems of cultural conflict and assimilation."[5] Las Casas's and Quiroga's first-hand investigation of Native Americans through the signs of humanity and culture they manifested formed the basis of imperial legislation framed by Vitoria's and Suarez's rethinking of natural law. Third, in contrast to Iberian scholasticism, the 'modern' philosophical tradition, exemplified in Britain through the natural rights theorizing of Thomas Hobbes (1588-1679) and John Locke (1632-1704), provided a simplistic justification for conquest of a 'natural' New World much as that of René Descartes (1596-1650) enabled man to embark on a crusade against a new natural world.

At first, however, when the Spanish encountered the Amerindians, they too made an intellectual effort to destroy them as human beings in theory so that in practice they could be mercilessly exploited or exterminated. Consider the caption of an anonymous woodcut

[4] Ibid. 42.

[5] W. Eames, trans., "Description of a Woodcut Engraving, Illustrative of the American Indians," *Bulletin of the New York Public Library 36* (1922), 755.

of 1505. It states Amerindians "go naked, both men and women," "have no personal property, but all things in common. . .without a king, and without a government."[6] Such descriptions sometimes evoked innocence, but in this case, as was more usual, they signified barbarism: "they take for wives whom they first meet. . . . They also war with each other, without art or rule. And they eat one another, and those they slay are eaten." Or, in the words of a foe of Las Casas, Gonzalo Fernandez de Oviedo y Valdes, who wrote in 1519, the Indians were "naturally lazy and vicious, melancholic, cowardly, and in general a lying, shiftless people. . . . They are idolatrous, libidinous, and commit sodomy. Their chief desire is to eat, drink, worship heathen idols, and commit bestial obscenities." [7] Nudity, stupidity, brutality, and cannibalism served as adequate signifiers of the Indians' otherness for those who wished to enslave or extirpate them.

Iberian defenders of Indian and human rights, on the contrary, soon began to counter this dehumanization of the New World "other." Significantly, they were the peninsula's leading philosophers or clerics trained in their tradition rather than conquistadors and their apologists. Dominican friar Antonio de Montesinos in 1511 preached a sermon on the Biblical text "I am a voice crying in the wilderness" in Spain's chief colony at that date, Hispanola. "Are these not men? Have they not rational souls? Are you not bound to love them as yourselves?" was Montesinos's response to the brutality which within fifty years would assist European diseases in wiping out an initial Indian population on the island of between one and several millions to the last person.[8]

Protests such as his won out. The first set of "New Laws" promulgated by Spain in 1512 forbade Indian slavery, beating Indians, and, significantly, calling them "perro [or any other name unless it

[6] Louis Hanke, *The Spanish Struggle for Justice in the Conquest of America* (2d. ed.: Boston: Little, Brown, 1949), 11.

[7] Ibid. 17.

[8] Louis Hanke, *Aristotle and the American Indians: A Study in Race Prejudice in the New World* (2d. ed.: Bloomington: Indiana University Press, 1959), 15.

is their proper name]."[9] The crown recognized that the name we bestow on someone affects our estimation of that person. Yet while royal policy operated on enlightened theory, it was impossible to enforce halfway around the world. One viceroy who tried to restrain exploitation was killed by Spaniards in Peru. In 1550, Domingo de Santo Tomas objected in Lima that the Indians were treated "as though they were brute animals and even worse than asses."[10]

To improve the treatment of Indians, their defenders had to show that Indian societies followed natural law and thus were entitled to be treated as human beings. They could do this in two ways: either demonstrating the moral superiority of the Indian way of life over the Spaniards, or showing that the two shared similar signs of a common humanity. The first, while gaining sympathy and periodically resurfacing in anti-colonial debates through the centuries, has ultimately proven futile as pre-Columbian cultures, like those which supplanted them, were by no means utopias. The argument for moral equality in spite of differences has proven more successful, and is as philosophically compelling as that of aboriginal superiority is untenable.

Perhaps the first major, systematic effort to associate Indians with natural law, and the Spanish with its violations, came from Vasco de Quiroga. He arrived in Mexico as an oidor, or judge, in 1530. At once the Spaniards' cruelty angered him.[11] In 1535, he wrote his magnum opus the *Informacion en Derecho del Licenciado Ouiroga Sobre Algunas Provisiones del Real Consejo de Indias* or *Legal Opinions Concerning Some Decrees of the Royal Council of the Indies* which the previous year had reinstituted slavery for Indians who resisted Spanish authority.[12] The rationale for this change—reversed again with the "New Laws" of 1542 following a papal bull of 1537 and much clerical protest—was that Spaniards would not wage "just

[9] Ibid. 27.

[10] Fintan Warren, *Vasco de Quiroga and His Pueblo-Hospitals of Santa Fe* (Washington: American Academy of Franciscan History, 1963), 26-42.

[11] Ibid. 30.

[12] Hanke, *Spanish Struggle for Justice* 92; idem., *Aristotle and the American Indians* 19.

wars" against the heathens unless they could enjoy the advantage of enslaving them.[13]

Quiroga reversed the way Indians and Spaniards were signified. Once freed from warrior societies like the Aztecs by the Spanish conquest, the Native Americans lived "simply, humbly, obediently," content with the little required for their daily needs in the manner of the Apostles and early Christians. Quiroga hoped to use the Indians to fulfill his dream of recreating the beauty and simplicity of the primitive church which had been lost forever in a corrupted Europe. Protected from all except carefully regulated contact with the Spaniards, the Indians would show their erstwhile conquerors the path to the true faith and proper moral behavior, reversing the general opinion of who was converting whom. Quiroga went on at length to show that the Indians lived in the "age of gold" described by the Latin poet Lucan whereas the Spaniards had deteriorated to the "age of iron"—an ironic comment on the iron weapons used to conquer a land valued primarily for its gold. Quiroga argued that the Spaniards were obliged to appear as true signifiers of the Christian philosophy of natural law if they wished to proselytize effectively. Thomas More's recently published *Utopia* idealizing a society without class distinctions based on wealth or private property, was Quiroga's ideal social and political organization for the Indians.[14]

The principal philosophical source Quiroga used to bolster his empirical evidence was Cardinal Cajetan's commentaries on Thomas Aquinas, published in 1517. The first of two key texts he cites is Cajetan's comment that "words and examples—or signs—must be used to convert the infidel. Cajetan argues that pagan rulers also derive their authority from God, and that attempts to convert non-Christians cannot excuse a "just war." "Jesus Christ, the king of kings, who had total power over Heaven and earth, did not send soldiers

[13] Vasco de Quiroga, *Informacion en Derecho del Licenciado Quiroga Sobre Algunas Provisiones Consejo de Indias* ed. C. J. Peredo (Mexico City: Secretaria de Educacion Publica, 1935), 188-204.

[14] Quoted in Spanish in Quiroga, *Informacion en Derecho* 69-71, 139-140. See also notes 25, 37, 38 below.

to conquer the world with weapons, but saintly preachers, as lambs among wolves." This was precisely Quiroga's plan to Christianize the Tarascan Indians, whose ferocity had protected them from both the Aztecs and Spaniards. Cajetan's second text which Quiroga cites maintains that Christians have no right to enslave pagans or barbarians. Instead, they must free them from their own tyrannical rulers.[15]

Quiroga's image of the "noble savage," combining Christian, classical, and Renaissance idealizations of the Indians' character, was as one-sided as his adversaries' counter-image. Yet it fairly described the decimated population he found in the 1530s, shocked into lethargy by conquest, disease, and mistreatment. In contrast, the Aztecs' human sacrifices and brutal wars against their neighbors, which the first conquistadors had observed a mere fifteen years earlier, lent credence to demonic images of the natives. As historian Anthony Pagden has criticized Quirog, the bishop erroneously viewed Indian society as morally pure yet politically unformed based on an abnormal situation characterized by disease, exploitation, and psychological strain.[16] Quiroga's supposition of a pre-civil state of nature required the Spaniards to institute a true government. If his theory led to uncritical praise of the Indians' moral character, it still branded them as the "other"—simple, childlike, and in need of benevolent education to learn to live in civilized society.

Quiroga practiced what he preached. In 1536, as Mexico's second bishop, he journeyed to Michoacan, high in the mountains some two hundred miles west of Mexico City. There he converted the Tarascans. Attracting them at first with beautiful music played and sung by monks and converted Indians, he established a reasonable approximation of his Utopia at Patzcuaro.[17] To this day, the workshops he founded survive and produce beautiful engraved

[15] Anthony Pagden, *Spanish Imperialism and the Political Imagination* (New Haven: Yale University Press, 1990), 26-28.

[16] Warren, *Quiroga* 43-58.

[17] James A. Sandos, "Junipero Serra's Canonization and the Historical Record," *American Historical Review 93*(1988), 1253-1269.

plates, stone sculptures, and other "artesanias" the Indians developed under the tutelage of the religious orders. A striking mural of Quiroga surrounded by Indians working at crafts and incorporating a picture of Thomas More holding a copy of his *Utopia* may be viewed in the town library.

Quiroga's attempt to keep the Indians separate from all Spaniards except the clergy and those Europeans under their supervision also bore fruit. It became the model for occupation of large parts of Latin America, notably the Jesuit settlements in Paraguay and Junipero Serra's chain of California missions. (Still, we must recognize even benevolent missions forced—and that is the correct word—widely dispersed populations to concentrate in missions where they died, through no fault of the padres, by the thousands in epidemics).[18] To this day the people of Michoacan are fiercely independent, predominantly Indian, and largely in possession of their own lands. They have given Mexico its great populist President Lazaro Cardenas (1934-1940) and his son Cuauhtemoc—named for the last Aztec emperor who led a revolt against the Spanish in 1521. He ran for President of Mexico in 1988 and would have won an honest election.

Similarly, Quiroga's assertion of the superiority of Indian culture to that of its exploiters has been reflected in many Latin American indigenismo movements in politics and literature. For instance, in the late twentieth century, Nicaraguan priest, poet, and Sandinista revolutionary Ernesto Cardenal has centered much of his work, such as the long poem "With Walker in Nicaragua," on the contrast between the unspoiled, healthy, pleasant signs of Indian society—signified by music, breezes, and cool color—and the signs of war, regimentation, and physical and spiritual degeneration—represented by grays, blacks, blood, and harsh odors—brought by the whites.[19]

Yet anyone who seriously investigates Native or Latin American

[18] Ernesto Cardenal, *With Walker Nicaragua and Other Poems* trans. J. Cohen (Middletown: Wesleyan University Press, 1988), 42-71.

[19] Quoted in Hanke, *Spanish Struggle for Justice* 11.

societies can point out the problem with such arguments. For all their attractiveness to those alienated with modernity, Native Americans warred against, exploited, tortured, and even ate each other. Latin America, despite its cultural wonders, has been wrought with vicious political warfare of the sort that enables Walker and his small band of men to become a meaningful force in Nicaragua at all. The argument that the Indians were people like us—no more, no less—is far more persuasive in arguing that they practiced and were also subject to natural law.

Unlike Quiroga and his successors, Las Casas did not argue that Indians were superior to whites, and thus entitled to be protected in carefully supervised communities or to serve as exemplars. To be sure, from time to time, he would note that "God created these simple people without evil and without guile. They are most obedient and faithful to their natural lords and to the Christians whom they serve. They are most submissive, patient, and virtuous. . . . They neither possess nor desire to possess worldly wealth."[20] But he did not convert this into an explicit claim of superiority. Las Casas generally relied on an image of Native Americans transcending either demonization or romanticization, especially in his famous 1550-1551 debate with the Aristotelian scholar Juan Gines de Sepulveda (1490-1573), one of the most admired classical scholars in Spain who had recently translated Aristotle's *Politics* and studied in Italy with that philosopher's great champion Pietro Pomponazzi. While it is impossible to reconstruct exactly what Sepulveda and Las Casas said in the debate, it is reasonable to assume they reiterated the points made in their major writings.[21]

Sepulveda's learning was his downfall in this debate as to whether Indians ought to be enslaved. He concentrated on the passage in Book 1, Chapter 6 of Aristotle's *Politics* where the Greeks termed all

[20] Las Casas' major writings are excerpted in English in G. Sanderlin, ed., *Bartolmé de las Casas: A Selection of His Writing* (New York: Alfred A. Knopf, 1947); Sepulveda's arguments are quoted in Hanke, *Aristotle and the American Indians* 47-52; see more generally 28-73.

[21] Hanke, *Aristotle and the American Indians*, 47.

barbarians or non-Greeks slaves "by nature," as fit to be ruled by their "natural" masters as the body was by the soul. Sepulveda then used the arguments typically put forth by the defenders of Indian slavery to justify their position. "Compare then those blessings enjoyed by the Spaniards of prudence, genius, magnanimity, temperance, humanity, and religion with those of the homunculi in whom you will scarcely find even vestiges of humanity, who not only possess no science but who lack letters and preserve no monument of their history except certain vague and obscure reminiscences of some things in certain paintings. Neither do they have written laws, but barbaric institutions and customs. They do not even have private property."[22]

One hears in Sepulveda's voice the same ideological fanaticism which in the twentieth century has demonized Communists, capitalists, blacks, Jews, etc. Piling up the adjectives to praise his own kind and demean "others," Sepulveda sought to appeal to Spanish pride despite the absurdity of his claim. He thinks in terms of absolute and abstract dichotomies. There is no investigation of what real Indians were doing at all. Not only had Sepulveda never been to the New World, as Las Casas tellingly points out, but he lumps all Indians and their cultures together without a second thought as Aristotle did with the barbarians. Indians are to whites "as children are to adults, as women are to men. Indians are as different from Spaniards as cruel people are from mild people."[23]

Despite his veneration for Aristotle, Sepulveda has no understanding of his master's method of carefully examining the advantages and disadvantages of different political systems and comparing them. He takes one section of Aristotle's work, the small section on slavery in the *Politics* treats this highly debatable and I believe usually misinterpreted passage—Aristotle talks about how the Greeks denote the barbarians as "natural slaves" without necessarily endorsing this notion—as a clear, sacred text, and

[22] Ibid. 52.
[23] Ibid. 47.

uncritically asserts the truth of a variety of abstract claims about Indians to prove they are fit for slavery.

Like modern supporters of imperialism, Sepulveda argues that the Spaniards greatly benefited the people they conquered. Wheat, barley, horses, mules, oxen, hogs, sheep, and any number of flora and fauna—which occupied land and consumed nutrients previously used to keep Indians alive—more than repaid the Indians for the gold and silver they mined. Sepulveda saw no irony in singling out iron—which the Indians experienced primarily in the form of weapons of destruction—as an especially valuable gift.[24] It was second only to the Christian faith, which he insisted could only be effectively preached once the Indians were conquered and set to work under Spanish supervision, despite the success of Quiroga's experiment in peaceful conversion and a comparable one by Las Casas in Chiapas—another region in Mexico where indigenous people continue to assert their rights to this day.

It is no wonder that Las Casas won the debate. The Council of the Indies and the King of Spain ruled against Indian slavery. Like the various declarations of human rights in our own day that condemned the exploitation of the many for the benefit of the few, this decree did not create a perfect world. It can even be argued that such pronouncements are insincere gestures which allow their elite authors to think they have done their duty and can thus put the problem out of their minds. But in ways which cannot be measured, the activities of some government officials and the religious orders, combined with the prohibition of outright enslavement, contributed to better conditions in Latin America at some times for some people. Nevertheless, the fact of the Zapatista rebellion in Chiapas, Mexico, began in 1994, testifies that the attempted destruction of indigenous peoples in the name of civilization persists despite the philosophical case supporting it.

Philosophically, the opposition between Sepulveda and Las Casas,

[24] Cardinal Cajetan (Tommaso de Vio), *Analogy of Names* trans. F. Koren (Pittsburgh: Duquesne University Press, 1953), cbs. 1-3.

or between imperialism and respect for natural law in dealing with other peoples, may be put in terms of Cajetan's theory of analogies, which had been current for about fifty years when Sepulveda and Las Casas debated. Sepulveda applied the "analogy of inequality" to show divisions between Indians and Europeans comparable to those between beasts and human beings. Las Casas invoked instead the "analogy of proportionality," where we can only learn about something—Cajetan used God's wisdom as an example—if some analogous relation exists between our traits and those we seek to understand.[25] The most important of these similar traits is a common humanity which requires a common practice of natural law.

Las Casas does not rest his argument against Indian slavery on the fact that Indians are superior and we have much to learn from them, or that we are corrupting the morals of the innocent. He rather insists they have more or less the same human and societal characteristics as Europeans and that with rare exceptions no justification exists for slavery of any sort anywhere. "The entire human race is one: all men are alike with respect to their creation and the things of nature. . . .All the races of the world have understanding and will and that which results from these two faculties in man—that is, free choice. And consequently, all have the power and ability and capacity. . . to be instructed, persuaded, and attracted to order and reason and laws, and virtue and all goodness."[26]

To support these claims, Las Casas uses empirical evidence to show Amerindians are no more barbaric and primitive than Spaniards: the two societies have comparable merits and defects. "What appears without doubt to exceed all human genius. . . is that art which those Mexican peoples have so perfectly mastered, of making from natural feathers. . . anything that they or any other first-class painters can paint with brushes." Improvements in this art following the conquest foreshadowed what Las Casas hoped would be the creative fusion of European and Indian culture in

[25] Las Casas, *Summary History of the Indies* ch. 48, reprinted in Sanderlin, *Las Casas.*
[26] Ibid. chs. 42, 62, 63.

many realms: "Granted that before we Christians entered there they made perfect and wonderful things by this art. . . so skillfully that the object appears alive or natural . . . yet after the Spaniards went there and they saw our statues and other things, they had occasion to branch out, to practice, and to distinguish themselves and that new and delicate art of theirs," the creation of religious artifacts out of feathers. A similar syncretism appears in the marvelous chapel at Tonantzintzla, built in the sixteenth century but still surviving, where wooden representation of saints who resemble pre-Columbian deities decorate the church with the same spectacular abundance as the blinding silver decor of the Chapel of the Convent of San Francisco in nearby Puebla, or in the flower designs on the engraved plates produced at Patzcuaro. Christianity and Spanish culture ideally would complement traits inherent in Indian society rather than contradict them.[27] Las Casas' hopes have been revived in the twentieth century by José Vasconcelos and others who found in Mexico's mixed mestizo "cosmic race" an improved fusion of Indian and European traits.

Similarly, Las Casas maintains that the Indians ruled themselves admirably before the Spanish came. In Cuzco in Peru and in Tenochtitlan (Mexico City) "were many million of people. . . . When we entered there, would we have found great unions of peoples in their towns and cities if they had lacked the order of a good way of life, peace, concord, and justice?" Citing Aristotle against Sepulveda to demonstrate the weakness of his opponent's case even on its own terms, Las Casas stated: "No republic or city can be preserved or can last, nor can a multitude of men live together, without the said virtues, as is apparent from the Philosopher's Ethics and Politics and as is manifest to every prudent man"—the last clause an obvious reference to Sepulveda's thoughtless and irrelevant parroting of so great a philosopher. Las Casas' conclusion: "Would to God, that in temporal affairs, Spain had been as well governed as

[27] Las Casas, "Letter to Fray Bartolomé Miranda de Carranza (1555)," partially reprinted in Sanderlin, *Las Casas*, 193.

the Indies and had such a good way of life," is hardly necessary to prove his case for Indian equality, although it supported his point that nearly all Spaniards should be banned from the New World as sources of disorder.[28] It is also required Spaniards to reflect on the moral deficiencies of their own history, and the great disorders which preceded the union of Castille and Aragon in 1492.

Nevertheless, Las Casas is not insisting on Amerindian superiority. If the Aztecs and Incas had superior political systems, the moral order of the Europeans, embracing the Christian religion, was a countervailing point. Las Casas' most interesting and powerful arguments for the equality of peoples involved his examination of the term "barbarism" and his daring justification of even the Indians' most objectionable practice—human sacrifice. Here he proves his greatness as a philosophical thinker. He does so by demonstrating the illegitimacy of Sepulveda's sleight-of-hand reasoning which would transform human similarities into differences.

Las Casas contradicts Sepulveda's blanket characterization of Indians as "barbarians" by distinguishing four kinds of barbarism.[29] First are people who "somehow become or are fierce, hard-hearted, and cruel," who "rush to commit acts so savage that wild beasts from the forests would not do worse. . . who seem to have stripped themselves completely of their human nature." This type of barbarism "results from chance, not nature." It thus could not be the basis for branding an entire group of people "natural slaves," since "such defects could not naturally befall an entire race."

A second sort of barbarians have a language or accent which strikes another group as strange or incomprehensible. "From this point of view, there is no man nor race which is not barbarous with respect to some other man or race. . . . Just as we esteemed these people of the Indies barbarous, so they considered us." Las Casas here considers Amerindian and European judgments of each other

[28] The following four arguments are found in Las Casas, *Summary History* chs. 264-267, in Sanderlin, ed. *Las Casas.*

[29] Las Casas, *History of the Indies*, Book 3, chs. 149-151, reprinted in Sanderlin, ed., *Las Casas.*

equally valid, or rather equally prejudiced. Perceiving cultural differences as badges of inferiority is a widespread though pernicious human trait. It cannot be used to argue the validity of one such set of perceptions over another.

The only barbarians whom Las Casas agrees fit Aristotle's definition of "slaves by nature" are people who "neither have nor care for law, right, nation, friendship, or the company of other men." They "do not live socially, and so they neither have nor endure lords, or laws, or political rule." This clearly does not apply to Indians with "their kingdoms and their kings, their way of life, their well-governed and well-ordered republics, their houses and estates," although the British philosophers Hobbes and Locke ignored precisely such evidence and arguments to brand all Indians as living in a "state of nature" and thus fit to be displaced.

Finally, barbarians may be considered those "who lack true religion and the Christian faith." But by such logic, even Aristotle and the Greeks who provided Sepulveda with his definition would be barbarians themselves and fit objects of slavery, "however wise or prudent they may be as philosophers and statesmen."

Expanding upon Aristotle, Las Casas thus offers us definitions of barbarism which with equal validity can be applied to the Spaniards (definitions one and two) or the Greeks themselves (definition four). For practical purposes, slaves by nature occur so rarely as to be irrelevant to any justification of slavery. The solitary madmen Las Casas grants are indeed natural slaves are so few, not to mention practically useless at taking directions and performing labor, that he is basically offering a general critique of slavery. Given "the Philosopher's" prestige, Las Casas could probably not say to the collected learned men of Spain what he had in an earlier clash of principles in 1519: that Aristotle was "a gentile burning in Hell, whose doctrine we do not need to follow except in so far as it conforms with Christian truth."[30] But he could create a philosophical new world which matched the geographical New World by using

[30] Ibid. Book 3, ch. 129.

a natural law critique to undermine the harsh exploitation of non-white people which accompanied the discovery of America.

In his mature thought, Las Casas argued against Negro slavery as well. He begged divine forgiveness for having erroneously been duped earlier in life by propaganda that blacks were captured in just wars in Africa and thus merely transferred while already slaves from African to European masters, who could at least teach them the true faith. "Since the Negroes themselves see that the Portuguese desire and seek them so eagerly, they wage unjust wars among themselves and in other illicit ways steal and sell each other to the Portuguese. Thus we are the cause of all the sins they commit against each other, as well as our own in buying them."[31]

Las Casas establishes a common humanity among Europeans and other peoples through common activities such as language, religion, and government in short, through their common adherence to natural law. Human sacrifice is perhaps the most startling yet effective sign Las Casas uses to show the Indians' humanity and equality rather than difference and barbarity. He does this by tracing a long history of human sacrifice among people of the ancient world otherwise considered civilized. Thus, "even though the Indians cannot be excused in the sight of God for worshipping idols, yet they can be excused completely in the sight of men." The grounds are what Aristotle, in the *Rhetoric* Book 1, chapter 20, termed "probable error." For social survival, Aristotle argued, "that must necessarily be judged to be good or better which is so judged by all," as in a society where human sacrifice is an unquestioned custom. Las Casas therefore notes that "it would not be right to make war on them for this reason both because. . . it is difficult for them to absorb in a short time the truth proclaimed to them through messengers and also because the Indians are under no obligation to believe the Spaniards." For the Spanish, while claiming to be civilized Christians, did not present themselves as such to the Indians: "Why will they believe

[31] Las Casas, *Defense Against Persecutors and Slanderers of the Peoples of the New World Discovered Across the Ocean* partially reprinted in Sanderlin, ed., *Las Casas*, 186-192.

such a proud, greedy, cruel, and rapacious nation?" Las Casas asked, applying to his countrymen the characteristics with which Sepulveda branded the Indians. "Why will they give up the religion of their ancestors, unanimously approved for so many centuries and supported by the authority of their teachers, on the basis of a warning from a people whose words work no miracles to confirm the faith or lessen vice?" Natural law is a historical and temporal, as well as an abstract, phenomenon. Until the Spaniards themselves appeared as genuine practitioners of the Christian religion they were in fact betraying through evil behavior, the Indians were justified in clinging to even the most "barbarous" practices. Las Casas thus juxtaposes Spanish and Indian cruelty. The difference is the Spanish are hypocritically violating their professed beliefs while the Indians are instead following theirs.[32]

The works of Las Casas, Quiroga, and numerous other defenders of the Indians described by historian Lewis Hanke powerfully affected the philosophy of the age as well as the Spanish missionary effort.[33] To be sure, we are not speaking of the tradition of Descartes, Locke, and Leibniz, but of the Thomist-influenced Spanish philosophy which culminated in John Poinsot's *Treatise on Signs.* Two of the greatest Spanish philosophers, Francisco di Vitoria[34] and Francisco Suarez[35], developed the idea of "ius gentium" or the law of nations, which maintains that all humanity was linked and defined by a natural or moral law, evidenced through reason and custom, established among all nations. (Respect for family and authority, prohibition of murder and theft are examples of this great unwritten code, simply yet beautifully expressed in modem times by C. S. Lewis in *The Abolition of Man.*)[36] Vitoria specifically illustrated the

[32] Hanke, *Spanish Struggle for Justice* 152-162.

[33] Francisco de Vitoria, *De Indis* and *De lure Belli*, in Vitoria, *Political Writings* trans. and ed., A Pagden and J. Lawrence (Cambridge: Cambridge University Press, 1991).

[34] Francisco Suarez, *Legibus* and *De Triplici, Virtute Theologica, Fide, Spe, et Charitate* in *Selections from Three Works of Francisco Suarez* (2 vols.: Oxford: Clarendon Press, 1944).

[35] C. S. Lewis, *The Abolition of Man* (New York: Macmillan, 1947.)

[36] The passage is from Book 2, Part 2, question 66, chapter 2, question 66, article 8 of Cajetan's 1517 *Commentaries Thomas Aquinas.* Vitoria cites this passage in *De*

"ius gentium" using American examples in *De Indis.* He and Suarez both denounced slavery—except as an individual penalty for criminals—and wars of conquest.

It would require an article at least as long as this one to show connections among the late Thomist Spanish philosophers in their treatment of the Indians. But to cite a few prominent instances: Vitoria used the same passage from Thomas Aquinas and Cajetan Quiroga had employed four years previously to insist Indians could not be expected to convert to Christianity unless the gospel was preached peacefully, persistently and reasonably.[37]Perhaps Vitoria had read the *Informacion en derecho* upon its publication. Suarez then brings forth this very citation to refute Sepulveda's case for forcible conversion.[38] Suarez also cites Vitoria's *De Indis* and *De lure Belli* eighteen times in *De Triplici Virtute Theologica* to condemn unjust wars and militant crusades against the heathen. Far from sequestering themselves in the monasteries and universities, early modem Spanish intellectuals, members of religious orders, spoke out powerfully against contemporary injustices.

And what of John Poinsot, who is considered the first thinker to systematically develop a theory of signs and signification? Poinsot and his principal modern champion, John Deely,[39] have followed a natural law tradition which finds signs of moral coherence present in both the natural world and human society to distinguish semiotics from the semiologists and practitioners of deconstruction who deny such coherence. *The Treatise on Signs* is as close to a purely theoretical investigation as a work of philosophy is likely to be. Yet there are two passages, read in the context of the debate over the nature and treatment of Indians which so vexed the Iberian philosophers, which can be interpreted to support implicitly Las Casas's position on the common nature of humanity. First, Poinsot distinguished between

lure Belli, see his *Political Writings* 263-269.

[37] Suarez, *De Triplici Virtute* disp. 8, sect 3-4.

[38] John Deely, *Four Ages of Understanding* (Toronto: University of Toronto Press, 2001).

[39] John Poinsot, *Tractatus de Signis: The Semiotic of Poinsot* trans. and ed. J. Deely and R. Powell (Berkeley: University of California Press, 1985), Book 1, qu. 6.

"brute animals" and "human beings"—not among different sort of human beings—in their use of signs: "In the case of signs whose signification we do not know from the outset," such as hearing a lion roar for the first time, "we ourselves, no less than brutes, have need of custom. But we accustom ourselves through reason and discourse, whereas animals accustom themselves inasmuch as their memory is fortified by some ordered pluralities heard or known, as for example, a given name, especially if they are thence affected by some benefit of injury, when they remember it as something to flee or seek." "Reason and discourse" characterize all human beings and are denied to all brutes.[40]

But people also have need of custom to interpret signs. Poinsot notes that a sign arising from custom does not perish from "a mere suspension removing the institution, but from a suspension removing the multiplication of acts and frequency of use." To provide the most relevant example, for Indians to abandon their old religion would require effectively changing their entire way of life. This could not be accomplished "from the will alone, without any multiplication of acts."[41] Christianity as preached to the Indians without patience and examples of moral behavior by the Spaniards, merely after overturning Indian institutions, would be futile since we cannot change our customary modes of understanding simply at will, but require the meaningful and repeated presence of alternative significations. By asserting that all human beings are endowed with language and reason, and cannot be expected to adopt new systems of belief until these have been concretely manifested as signs consistent with natural law and appropriate to their customs and discourse, Poinsot provided a theoretical justification for the social philosophy of Las Casas and Quiroga.

Just as the Spanish philosophical tradition, proceeding in the scholastic mode of carefully and subtly examining correspondences and differences, led to a defense of the dignity of aboriginal peoples on the grounds of natural law, British philosophy precluded one. Each

[40] Ibid. Book 2, qu. 6.

[41] Bernard Bailyn, *The Origins of American Politics* (New York: Knopf, 1967).

system reflected its nation's circumstances. In Spain and Spanish America, a powerful church, military orders, urban corporations, and aristocracy alternatively vied with or supported each other and the crown in shifting coalitions. Economic development and property rights were subordinated to a system of intricate government regulation and societal relations. Rights of individuals and groups were complementary with obligations in a complex system which used natural law as its moral standard. In Britain, on the other hand, the basic struggle was between the House of Commons and the crown; the weakness of the established church, and its dependence on the monarch led religious dissent to reinforce political protest. British political thought was dualistic: good lay on one side, evil on the other. It was concerned with struggles between Parliament and King; court and country, power and liberty, or private corruption and civic virtue, reflected these struggles.[42] Ultimately, Parliament, the country, and liberty won. Virtue did not.

Britain, like its American successors, has always regarded its political heritage and relatively open economic system as a national treasure promoting freedom. But as historian Karen Kupperman writes, its by-products were less pleasant: a "contentious, selfish society" characterized by "naked greed" emerged from the "breakdown of the old community" through "the search for money and profit, in fact unrestricted capitalism." Under such conditions, in sixteenth and seventeenth century England, "masterless men looked for work. . . humble people found themselves squeezed as food prices rose disastrously"; "America was seen as a great sinkhole into which England's superfluous multitude could be sent."[43]

In short, Spain was a quasi-feudal society. Intricate relationships of mutual dependence and corporate legitimacy are mirrored in scholastic philosophy which assigned rights and responsibilities to everyone in society and balanced the various elements such as

[42] Karen Kupperman, *Settling with the Indians The Meeting of English and Indian Cultures in the Americas, 1580-1640* (Totowa: Rowman and Littlefied, 1980), 8, 135, 142.

[43] C. B. MacPherson, *The Political Theory of Possessive Individualism, Hobbes to Locke* (Oxford: The Clarendon Press, 1962).

body and soul or humanity and God. The social order perfected the natural order. In Britain, on the other hand, the greatest political philosophers, Hobbes and Locke based the social order on the twin principles that a natural order in which all warred against all (Hobbes) or at any rate feared for the safety of their property (Locke) had to be overcome. Men created the state voluntarily, like a commercial agreement, to preserve order by guaranteeing the "natural" rights to life (Hobbes) or life, liberty, and property (Locke). As C. B. McPherson has written in *The Political Theory of Possessive Individualism*,[44] British philosophy reflected British society that feared disorder and desired a state to protect a class system based on private control of property.

The manner in which Spain and Britain respectively occupied their American colonies also reflected their social systems. We remember Columbus's ceremony of landing with banners, even though where he landed is still disputed. The Spanish made sure to read elaborate texts to the natives to offer them peaceful Christianization before taking possession even when the Indians had no idea of what they were saying. For the British colonies, we remember places—Plymouth Rock, Jamestown—for settlers who simply aimed to take possession of land, rather than "articulating a relationship between Europeans and a living, breathing "Other," as did the Spanish.[45]

With respect to Hobbes and Locke, the Amerindians served the same purpose they did for the British colonists. They were an obstacle to be overcome as quickly as possible so that civilization could be established. They were cleared out of Hobbes' and Locke's texts so that the discussion, like the settlers (British America was "settled," Latin America "conquered"), could move on to civil society. Hobbes mentions Indians exactly three times in the ten-volume collection of

[44] Seed, "Taking Possession and Reading Texts: Establishing the Authority of Overseas Empires," *William and Mary Quarterly* 3d ser. (1992), 184, 209.

[45] Thomas Hobbes, *A Defense of True Liberty* reprinted in volume 3 of W. Molesworth, ed., *The English Works of Thomas Hobbes of Malmesbury* (10 vols. London, J. Bohri, 1839-1845), ch. 1, par. 13.

his works published in the nineteenth century. In his essay on *Liberty* "they of America" serve as examples of "perpetual war," of the state of nature, where people were "few, fierce, short-lived, poor, nasty, and deprived of all that pleasure and beauty of life, which peace and society are wont to bring them."[46]

Indians appear twice in Hobbes' masterpiece *Leviathan*: First, Hobbes uses them to prove that the terrible natural state characterized by the war of all against all really does exist: "For the savage people in many places of America, except the government of small families, the concord whereof dependeth on natural lust, have no government at all."[47] Second, Native Americans serve as examples "Of Darkness from Vain Philosophy, and Fabulous Traditions" in the chapter of that title. Admitting that "the savages of America, are not without some good moral sense; also they have a little arithmetic," they nevertheless "lived upon gross experience; there was no method; that is to say, no sowing nor planting of knowledge by itself, apart from the weeds, and common plants of error and conjecture."[48] Hobbes uses botanical metaphors to relegate Indians to a physical state of nature to accompany the pre-political one.

Locke, in his famous *Second Treatise of Government*, took more interest in America. After all, he drew up the first, abortive constitution of the Carolinas at the behest of his patron, proprietor Anthony Ashley Cooper, First Earl of Shaftesbury—South Carolina's two principal rivers, the Ashley and the Cooper, are still named for him. But Locke's primary interest in America is to prove that because the Indians have no property to protect—they appear to use only a minuscule proportion of their territory from a European perspective—their land is thus "waste" or "vacant" and can be possessed by the first civilized comers. The key text is paragraph 45 of the *Second Treatise of Government:* "Labor, in the beginning, gave a right of

[46] Thomas Hobbes, *Leviathan* reprinted in volume 2 of Molesworth, ed., Works of Thomas Hobbes part. 1, ch. 13.
[47] Ibid. part 4, ch. 46.
[48] John Locke, *Two Treatises of Government* P. Laslett, ed. (Cambridge: Cambridge University Press, 1960), *Second Treatise* pars. 45, 41.

property," but only "wherever any one was please to employ it." A social compact only exists "where men have, by positive agreement, settled a property amongst themselves in distinct parts and parcels of the earth." Where the inhabitants "not having joined with the rest of mankind, in the consent of the use of their common money," the lands therefore " waste and are more than the people, who dwell on it, do, or can make use of, and so still lie in common." Locke cannot imagine a life of sufficiency apart from the comforts of civilization: the Indians "are rich in land, and poor in all the comforts of life," although Nature has provided for "as liberally as any other people. . . yet for want of improving it by labor, have not one hundredth part of the conveniences we enjoy. And a king of a large fruitful territory there feeds, lodges, and is clad worse than a day laborer in England."[49]

Locke's use of Indians echoed excuses for dispossessing them offered by his countrymen. "The whole earth is the Lord's garden, and he hath given it to the sons of Adam to be tilled and improved by them," wrote John Winthrop, the leader of Puritan Massachusetts. "Why then should we stand starving here. . . and in the meantime suffer whole countries, as profitable for the use of man, to lie waste without any improvement?"[50] Abandoned villages and heaps of skeletons suggested that many North American natives had been carried off by disease spread by occasional contact before the first wave of settlement, confirming a common argument rearticulated as late as the 1770s by Benjamin Franklin in his *Autobiography* that it was "the design of Providence to extirpate these savages in order to make room for the cultivators of the earth."[51]

Like Winthrop and Franklin, Locke denies that the aboriginal inhabitants have any right to the land since they do not perform labor, from which all value comes. Not putting their land to commercial

[49] John Winthrop, "General Considerations for the Plantation in New England," quoted in Roy Harvey Pearce, *Savagism and Civilization: A Study of the Indian and the American Mind (*2d ed.: Berkeley: University of California Press, 1988), 21.
[50] Benjamin Franklin, *Autobiography* ed. J. A. L. Lemay and P. Zall (New Haven: Yale University Press, 1964), 108-109.
[51] Locke, *Second Treatise*, pars. 102, 108.

use, signified by money, means that "in many parts of America there was no government at all." The inhabitants "had neither kings nor commonwealth, but lived in troops, as they do this day" (c. 1690) in Florida, Brazil, and elsewhere. Only for purposes of war, when because "they have no certain kings," they "choose their captains as they please," can we discern the beginnings of civil society. Although such arrangements are temporary, Locke uses them to support his point that government begins with the consent of equals who band together for self-protection.[52]

Locke is noted as an empirical philosopher, and a founder of semiotics which implies the careful investigation of signs he performed in his strictly philosophical work;[53] but when dealing with Indian society, he threw empiricism out the window. His brief discussion is uninformed by common sense, knowledge of reality, or awareness of his own prejudices. If Indian societies were so impoverished, how could their assistance have made the difference between survival and death for many of the original white settlers? And Indians worked. Women labored at agriculture, creating value even though villages moved around to follow the game and avoid soil exhaustion. Hunting was neither an upper-class prerogative nor sport, as it was in England, but a form of work that required Indian men to travel long distances and carry back their prey. Territory was used, if less intensively than in more populated Europe.

Neither Hobbes nor Locke went beyond the blanket stereotyping of Indians that the Spanish defenders of enslavement employed. Indians only existed for them as negative signifiers of the main problem British society had to overcome—lack of order for Hobbes, lack of labor, commerce, and secure property for Locke. Like many British writers who had never visited the New World, Locke and Hobbes even ignored eyewitness accounts which amply demonstrated

[52] See the discussion in John Deely, "John Locke's Place in the History of Semiotic Inquiry," in J. Evans and J. Deely, eds., *Semiotics* 1986 (Lanham: University Press of America, 1987).

[53] Kupperman, *Settling with the Indians,* 46, 64, ch. 5.

that the British among the Indians found sophisticated systems of government, culture, religion, and technology well-adapted to the environment.[54] The first chroniclers of British settlement of North America, almost all of them possessing substantial commercial or landed wealth, did not even use racist language—Indians were not perceived as "red" until the mid- eighteenth century but basically as whites with somewhat darker skin tones who had been much exposed to the sun.[55] Rather, "colonists saw or feared all the same defects in their fellow Englishmen and women which they saw in Indians."[56] "The Indians were exploited, not because they were seen as so alien or inferior that they did not fit into any English categories, but because they fitted only too well into the mass of people at the bottom of society whose role it was to serve others." "Wild Irishmen" had preceded North American "savages."[57] Englishmen observed "a great many character defects and vices, ranging from improvidence, vengefulness, treachery, thievery, sexual promiscuity, all the way up to cannibalism" not only in America and Ireland; these were their greatest self-criticisms, especially applied to the lower class.[58]

Conversely, when seventeenth-century Englishmen "described Indian society, the characteristic on which they lavish the most praise was the great authority of the kings and the reverence of the governed for them."[59]As John Smith wrote of Virginia's Powhatan society: "Although the country be very barbarous, yet they have amongst them such government, as that their magistrates for good commanding, and their people for due subjection, and obeying, excel many places that would be counted very civil."[60] Admirable Indians

[54] Alden T. Vaughan, *The Roots of American Racism* (New York: Oxford University Press, 1996), 417-418.

[55] Kupperman, Settling with the Indians, 4.

[56] James Muldoon, "The Indian as Irishman," *Essex Institute Historical Collections 111*(1975), 267-289.

[57] Kupperman, *Settling with the Indians*, 140.

[58] Ibid.49, 121.

[59] John Smith, *A Map of Virginia*, quoted in Pearce, Savagism and Civilization 15.

[60] Kupperman, *Settling with the Indians*, 127.

had solved the very problem of political stability with which Anglo-American society struggled so mightily in early modem times.

When the English went to war against the Native Americans, the excuse given was treachery: "Of all the accusations made against the Indian, the most universal and perhaps the most serious was that he was treacherous."[61] Prompted by European encroachments on their land and scattered outrages, the "massacre" attempted by Virginia's Powhatans in 1622 brought an end to English reports which stressed the Indians' attractive appearance, courage, good government and helpful assistance. Then the negative characteristics took over. According to Rev. Samuel Purchas "so bad a people, having little of humanity but shape, ignorant of civility, of arts, of religion, more brutish than the beasts they hunt," justified comparable retaliation: they "hath now confiscated whatsoever remainders of right the unnatural Naturals had, and made both them and their country wholly English."[62] Similarly New England, which maintained generally good relations with its aboriginal inhabitants until King Philip's War in 1675-76 and even made a reasonable effort to Christianize them, justified the Pequot War of 1637 as just retaliation on a treacherous people. Alden T. Vaughan, the most important scholar of early New England-Indian relations, has found that "virtually all colonial commentators (English and Dutch) and most Indians (Narragansett, Mohegan, and the Connecticut River tribes) whose opinions are recorded concur that the Pequots were persistently belligerent and aggressive."[63] The invaders projected on the invaded an innate immorality more appropriate to themselves.

Whether natives or British were to blame for Virginia's and New England's changes of policy is not the issue here. The interesting point is that the charge made by the settlers, "treachery," or breach of a ratified peace, is a justification reflecting a society relying heavily

[61] Samuel Purchas, *Haklytus Posthumous or Purchas His Pilgrimes*, quoted in Pearce, *Savagism and Civilization*, 7 – 8.

[62] Vaughan, *Roots of American Racism,* 190.

[63] John Winthrop, "A Modell of Christian Charity," *The Winthrop Papers* (5 vols.: Boston: The Massachusetts Historical Society, 1929-1947), 2: 272-285.

on "covenants," or voluntary agreements among people, to further commerce and establish religious authority. John Winthrop's famous "City Upon a Hill" speech to the Puritans about to land in Massachusetts described the enterprise: "we are entered into covenant with Him for this work, we have taken out a commission, the Lord hath given us leave to draw up our own articles. . . if the Lord shall. . . bring us in peace to the place we desire. . . then He hath ratified this covenant and sealed our commission, and will expect a strict performance of the articles contained in it." Otherwise, he will "be revenged of such a perjured people, and make us know the price of the breach of such a covenant."[64] The language of commerce has become the voice of God and the excuse for destroying those who violated what the English saw as betrayal.

Neither American colonists—a few exceptions such as Roger Williams and William Penn aside—nor the British philosophers whose political theory of natural rights became the foundation of the modern, liberal, democratic state made any effort to defend the rights of Native Americans. Such a silence well suited the proto-capitalist economy developing in Anglo-America, which glorified labor, commerce, and property, and condemned sloth and waste. It also suited the closely connected Puritan doctrine which established a clear-cut division between the saved and the damned. Nature for the Puritans was a wilderness to be conquered, not the order of things based on natural law stressed by Thomas Aquinas and his successors. Divisions were sharp and simple, based on religious performance—saved or damned, no purgatory—or class—the propertied and the landless. Nature for Locke and Hobbes was an evil to be overcome, and government existed only to overcome the evils of pre political society. As Descartes separated spirit from nature and mind from body, the Indians, signified as natural and pre-political, existed only to be conquered, shunted aside, or exterminated in the interests of progress.

A bad argument can be made that since droves of British came to "settle" a relatively underpopulated region of America as opposed to a few Spaniards who "conquered" populous advanced societies rich in gold and

[64] Alfred Crosby, *The Columbian Exchange: Biological and Cultural Consequences of 1492* (Westport: Greenwood Press, 1972), 166.

silver, demography and geography rather than philosophy determined the respective response of the two nations to the peoples they subjugated. But would it have made any difference if the British had to sweep aside ten times as many Native Americans? In fact, recent estimates of the aboriginal population of North America north of Mexico at the time of settlement tend to place it much higher than has been traditionally thought, at about ten million in 1500 declining to one million by 1650—the respective figures for Latin America being fifty to one hundred million and twelve million.[65]As James Muldoon has written in his perceptive study of the writings of Juan de Solorzano Pereira (1575-1654)—yet another legal philosopher trained at Salamanca whose *De Indiarum Jure* (1629-1639) was the most prestigious treatise on the subject for over a century and a half-"the reason the Spanish could analyze and criticize the manner of the conquest of the New World so thoroughly was that they continued to perceive relations between Europeans and the non-European within the framework that medieval lawyers, philosophers, and theologians had created. They possessed a set of moral standards against which they could measure the activities of the conquistadors before passing judgment on them, as well as a language that could articulate their views."[66]

The Iberians' language and analysis was a complex mixture of theory and respect for fact, as opposed to the deductive British philosophers who ignored ample evidence and merely assumed Indians to be inferior. As Deely notes with respect to Poinsot, the Iberians based their judgments of the conquest on interpreting investigations conducted by men like Las Casas into the pasts and concrete activities of both Spaniards and Indians: They placed "historicity at the very center of human thought rather than, as the modem philosophers all but unanimously supposed, at the margins of what is understood."[66] History provides the evidence to determine whether philosophers, and the historical actors they defend, are telling the truth.

But it requires serious historical inquiry to bring to light the buried pasts of the vanquished. Iberian scholars who painstakingly refuted the vision of Amerindian societies spread by their conquerors that "savages" without government or order inhabited a "waste" have provided much of

[65] James Muldoon, *The Americas in the Spanish World Order: The Justification for Conquest in the Seventeenth Century* (Philadelphia: University of Pennsylvania Press, 1994), 170.

[66] John Deely, *New Beginnings: Early Modern Philosophy and PostModern Thought*,

the information that late twentieth century historians now use to reconstruct the nature of the pre-Columbian world. The early modern Spanish clergy anticipated the contemporary historical enterprise of "history from the bottom up" that scholars seeking alternative narratives to the "official stories" of princes and parliaments have undertaken, criticizing conquerors and validating the popular culture of oppressed peoples. By confirming the mutual interdependence of history and natural law, of praxis and thought, of matter and spirit, the school of Salamanca refuted in advance the terrible simplifiers, the false dichotomies Cartesian, Hobbesian, Lockean, and Puritan thinkers postulated as real to define a new world out of existence and excuse its subjugation.

Poinsot and his predecessors thereby place those who would trivialize the Iberian search for justice based on natural law in an absurd epistemological position. By asserting that economic, geographic, or demographic factors governed the course of colonization, the point to be proven has to be assumed as the starting point of the argument. Only by prejudging the life of the mind as irrelevant to a materialist universe can the differences between a conquest which discarded the losers and one which incorporated them be maintained.

This is not to say, of course, that in practice Iberian colonization was not exploitative and cruel. So was feudal society. What I am claiming is that the philosophical tradition of natural law was imported into Latin America to subject conquest to moral judgment, and that this tradition has informed thought and behavior—to an unmeasurable but very real degree down to the present. In contrast, the best of Anglo-American philosophy literally got rid of the Indians as quickly as possible so white people could compete for the right to take their land.

It is important that we realize the First World today confronts similar choices to those the colonists of Spain and Britain faced in the early modern era. As the United States is challenged with incorporating an ever-larger Hispanic population in the third millennium, and as national boundaries throughout the world prove increasingly unable to contain the unwanted "other," we have the option to revive the humane vision and rearticulate the historically generous method of Suarez, Vitoria, and Las Casas. By doing so, we can demonstrate that the life of the mind has a nobler purpose than to design the technical means and pseudo- philosophical justifications to allow the powers that be to extract more resources from a depleted planet and its impoverished population.

This article first appeared in *The International Journal of Applied Semiotics*, Vol. 5, Nos. 1 & 2. Reprinted with permission from Atwood Press and the author.

JOHN COURTNEY MURRAY AND ST. THOMAS AQUINAS ON OBEDIENCE AND THE CIVIL CONVERSATION

Paul J. Cornish

INTRODUCTION

The figure of John Courtney Murray looms large in the works of Catholic moral philosophers in the contemporary United States.[1] Academics and Catholic religious from a wide variety of ideological and religious perspectives seem to look for and find what they need in Murray's life and writings to support their own arguments. The present paper arises not from concerns about moral philosophy or theology or even from concerns about the compatibility of the American Constitution with Catholicism. It is motivated by an intellectual desire to move beyond contemporary preoccupations over the tension between freedom and obligation. As a political theorist I hope to find in Murray's a more eloquent account of the compatibility of our passion for individual freedom and the need to inspire citizens with a sense of civic duty. Does Murray provide a coherent account of the liberty of the citizen in a liberal republic?

Nearly fifty years ago Murray expressed concerns about the viability of the 'civil conversation' in the United States in his work *We Hold These Truths: Catholic Reflections on the American Proposition.*[2] Murray explained that the concept of a conversation arose from a twofold Latin sense of 'living together' and 'talking together.' A civil conversation requires the existence of a strong society that has advanced from a preoccupation with physical survival to a life of civilized pursuits. Murray believed that this kind of a civil society requires some sort of concord or 'conspiracy' that orients all members of the society to a common good based on a

[1] See for example the essays collected in *The Catholic Church, Morality and Politics* edited by Charles E. Curran and Leslie Griffin (New York: Paulist Press, 2001).

[2] See John Courtney Murray, *We Hold These Truths: Catholic Reflections on the American Proposition*, (New York: Sheed and Ward, 1960; reprinted by Rowman and Littlefield, 2005), 30-31, and the selections in *John Courtney Murray and the American Civil Conversation*, Robert P. Hunt and Kenneth L. Grasso, editors (Grand Rapids: Eerdmans, 1992). Richard J. Regan's, *The Moral Dimensions of Politics*, (New York: Oxford University Press, 1986) develops a contemporary account of civil discourse based in part on that of Murray. See Chapter 4, "Moral Good and Civic Good," 92-106.

moral consensus, which he called "the public consensus." Murray's work did not focus on the kind of practices that make this consensus practicable, but he did acknowledge that it had to be "laboriously cultivated by the discipline of passion, prejudice and narrow self-interest."

Murray described the substance of the American consensus in terms of Lincoln's "proposition" (that all men are created equal) at Gettysburg, and argued that it arose from a tradition of natural law predating *The Declaration of Independence* and traceable back to the works of St. Thomas Aquinas.[3] It appears then that Murray's concept of a civil conversation arises from his reflections on Aquinas's *Treatise on Law* (I-II 94, 2, corpus) dealing with the natural human inclinations and the precepts of natural law:

> … there is in man an inclination to good according to the nature of reason which is proper to him, as man has a naturalinclination to know the truth about God, to live in society and, in accord with this inclination all those things which relate to it belong to the Natural Law, namely, that a man avoid ignorance and that he should not offend others with whom he ought to live and similar things which relate to this inclination.[4]

[3] Murray's account of the American consensus includes five components: the conviction that the United States is a nation under God, the tradition of natural law, the principle of consent, the idea of a virtuous people, and the vindication of historical and human rights (2005, 43-57). Murray's account of the natural law tradition is interesting in itself, since it stresses the continual development of the natural law tradition from Aquinas into the British context and through Fortescue, Bracton and Blackstone into the colonies by the Founding Era (2005, 46-48). In this regard he seems to have been influenced by Clinton Rossiter's *Seedtime of the Republic* (New York: Harcourt, Brace, 1953) and by Edward S. Corwin's *The "Higher Law" Background of American Constitutional Law* (Ithaca, NY: Cornell University Press, 1955, c. 1929).

[4] Tertio modo inest homini inclination ad bonum secundum naturam rationis quae est sibi propia: sicut homo habet naturalem inclinationem as hoc quod veritatem cognoscat de Deo, et ad hoc quod societate vivat; et secundum hoc ad legem naturalem pertinent ea quae ad hujusmodi inclinationem spectant, utpote quod homo ignorantiam vitet, quod alios non offendat cum quibus debet conversari, et caetera hujusmodi quae ad hoc spectant. Translation and Latin text from St. Thomas Aquinas, *The Treatise of Law: Summa Theologiae I-II; qq. 90-97*, edited by R.J. Henle, S.J. (Notre Dame, IN: University of Notre Dame Press, 1993) 249-250. This threefold analysis of natural inclinations is an unattributed allusion to Cicero's *De officiis* I.11ff.

If, as I believe, Murray's argument about the civil conversation is an invocation of the natural inclination to live together and to talk together (*conversatio*) it refers to a conception of political life that is profoundly different from those contemporary versions of liberalism,[5] and even of some contemporary reinterpretations of Aquinas's natural law doctrine that see the good of political life as a good that is instrumental to other goods (the good of the family, for instance), or even dispensable in the pursuit of happiness.[6]

Murray's younger contemporary John Rawls constructed his theory of justice as fairness through the vehicle of the social contract. His approach exhibited a powerful concern over the need for a general theory of justice and legal obligation applicable to a pluralistic society. Aquinas's *Treatise on Law* is not concerned primarily with the justification of civil authority and legal obligation that preoccupy liberal political theorists. For Aquinas, law is understood to be an external cause of human actions, directing them towards ends to which people are naturally inclined so that they might attain virtue and temporal happiness. Aquinas understood these inclinations to be intellectual, in the sense that the human being as an intellectual creature experiences the good as intelligible.[7] He, like Aristotle, posits a natural inclination to virtue that must be developed through habituation and instruction.

Murray, like John Rawls, was concerned with the need for a public philosophy in an increasingly pluralistic, postmodern society. His work helped to bring about a convergence between the official political teaching of the Catholic Church and liberal democracy through the adoption of *Dignitatis humane,* the "Declaration of Religious Freedom" at the Second Vatican

[5] I have in mind especially the works of John Rawls.

[6] See John Finnis, *Aquinas: Moral, Political, and Legal Theory* (Oxford: Oxford University Press, 1998), especially Chapter VII, "The State: Its Elements and Purposes," (220-254) for an argument that Aquinas believed that political society is something less than a 'basic human good,' and that Aquinas believed that political society is instrumental to the instantiation of the basic good of 'society' in the household and the religious community. For a cogent critique of Finnis's account as an interpretation of Aquinas, see Lawrence Dewan, O.P. "St. Thomas, John Finnis, and the Political Good," *The Thomist*, 64 (2000) 337-74.

[7] Brock, Stephen L. "Natural Inclination and the Intelligibility of the Good in Thomistic Natural Law," *Vera Lex* (2005) VI.1-2, 57-78.

Council.

In what follows I develop an understanding of the concept of a civil conversation as it is treated by Murray and in the works of St. Thomas Aquinas. My central contention is that Murray's understanding of the need for a renewed civil conversation is tied to the doctrine that there are natural human inclinations to know the truth about God and to live in conversation with others. For this reason it is a serious deprivation for human beings not to live in a true civil community, and not to participate in an ongoing civil conversation.

In the sections of the essay that follow I will make some brief and preliminary observations about the term *conversatio* as it appears in Aquinas. I will then turn to an account of the civil conversation in Aquinas. My account derives in part from Murray's insight about the relevance of natural law for contemporary life. He argues that the political teachings of natural law may be understood in terms of an empirical situation:

> Consider, for instance, the contents of the consciousness of a man who is protesting against injustice, let us say, in a case where his own interests are not touched and where the injustice is wrought by technically correct legislation. The contents of his consciously protesting mind would be something like these. He is asserting that there is an idea of justice; that the idea is transcendent to the actually expressed will of the legislator; that it is rooted somehow in the nature of things; that he really *knows* this idea; that it is not made by his judgment but is a measure of his judgment; that its violation is injury, which his mind rejects as unreason; that this unreason is an offense not only against his own intelligence but against God, Who commands justice and forbids injustice. [8]

The problem of injustice, so stated, raises a question about how one is to determine whether or not to obey human authorities. With this in mind, my account of the civil conversation will focus on

[8] Murray, *We Hold These Truths*, 294 (emphasis in the original)

two key passages in which the issue of human inclinations to the good arise: in the question on the virtue of obedience (2-2, 104) as compared to parallel passages in other works, and in the question on the precepts of natural law (1, 94, 2). It also will be necessary to consider the virtue of obedience in relation to the cardinal virtues of justice and prudence, and to the virtue of charity.

In the final section of the work I will review some contemporary trends convergent with Murray's concern about the civil conversation. I describe a situation in which any attempt to reconstruct a public philosophy for the contemporary United States should deemphasize theories of obligation and turn to a renewed emphasis on human purpose, human excellence, and the pursuit of happiness. However pluralist a society becomes, it still requires a conversation about the purposes it will undertake as a community, and their compatibility with natural law and human dignity. The citizens' willingness to discipline their passions depends upon an inspiring vision of the civil conversation.

THE MEANINGS OF *CONVERSATIO*

The Latin noun *conversatio* is not easily rendered into English. The first meaning given by standard Latin/English lexicons is 'social intercourse'. This translation is awkward but captures the diverse connotations of the concept. In living together human beings develop multiple and interrelated practices and languages having to do with living and living well together. In his standard reference work, *A Lexicon of St. Thomas Aquinas*, Deferrari adds the second synonym "association," and points out that the term is used in Latin as a synonym of *communicatio*, *communio*, and *communitas*. A further definition is 'conduct'or 'way of life'.

St. Thomas posits that human beings are inclined to conversation, or communion, with other people and all intellectual beings. There are indeed, multiple levels and varieties of conversation discussed in his works. His conception of beatitude is salvation in the sense of communion with God, but also with the entire church. Human society includes the domestic conversation of the household, the civil conversation of the political community, and the spiritual conversation of the church or religious community. The term social intercourse also connotes economic life in the sense of trade, contract and commercial society. In the high medieval society of 13th century Europe Aquinas would have been aware of the way that corporate entities like cities, universities, guilds and religious orders constituted specialized conversations of their own. Indeed his participation in public debates about whether the members of mendicant orders should occupy chairs at the University of Paris was a formative event in his professional life.[9]

It is clear from many passages in Aquinas's work that he understands sociability to be a vital cause in the development of virtue. Returning to the passage from the *Treatise on Law* quoted above, he argues that natural law includes precepts that teach us not to give offense to the people with whom we live and converse. Compare the anthropology of the political community one finds in Aristotle's *Politics* and Cicero's *De officiis*,[10] with Aquinas's work, *On Kingship*:

> For nature has in the case of other animals provided food, fur covering, means of defense … But human beings have been constituted with none of these things provided by nature. Rather human beings have instead been provided reason, which enables them to provide all these things for themselves by the work of their hands. But a single human being does not suffice to provide all these things, since single human beings by themselves could not adequately make their way through life. Therefore it is natural for human beings to live in community with many.[11]

[9] Aquinas composed his polemical work *Contra impugnantes Dei cultum religionem* (1256) during his first year of magisterial teaching at Paris to counter arguments of members of the faculty at the University of Paris who argued that the members of new mendicant orders should not be allowed to such positions. See Jean-Pierre Torrell, O.P. *Saint Thomas Aquinas: Volume I, The Person and His Work* (Washington: Catholic University Press, 1996) 75ff.

[10] *Politics* I.2, 12, 1252^{a}24ff, and *De officiis* I.11ff.

[11] Aliis enim animalibus natura praeparavit cibum, tegumenta pilorum, defensionem, ut dentes, cornua, ungues vel saltem velocitatem as fugam. Homo autem institutus est nullo

In the subsequent passage Aquinas goes on to explain the way that human beings need each other in order to learn how to survive, but also to develop virtue. Unlike other animals that have 'indigenous structures' that allow them to identify healthy foods and recognize enemies, human beings must learn through experience. Since it is impossible for a single human being to develop knowledge of all that is needed, we learn from each other and depend on each other. One learns about medicine, another about building materials, and so on. What is more, human beings need moral virtue to live well, and prudence is integral to all of the moral virtues since it involves choosing well. Since prudence arises through experience, and we cannot experience everything we must learn to develop complete virtue, we need to experience the examples and expertise of others in an ongoing process of self-disclosure, a conversation.

For Aquinas the virtue of justice is "the constant and perpetual will to render to others what is due them." Justice, according to Aquinas, "orders the activities of other virtues to its own end by moving them by its command."[12] Thus many special virtues are connected to justice because of the social nature of the human good. For example, without trust society is impossible, so Aquinas associates conversation and living together (*convivere*) with the need for the virtue of truth. The virtue of truth, or truthfulness, refers especially to one's willingness to present oneself as he truly is and without exaggeration or suppression.[13] Society requires order, so people need to follow customary rules and laws. This involves the virtue of obedience. These and related virtues are addressed by Aquinas in a series of articles in the *Summa Theologiae* to which

---

horum sibi a natura praeparato, sed loco omnium data est ei ratio, per quam sibi haec omnia officio manuum posset praparare ad quae omnia praeparanda unus homo non sufficit. Nam unus homo per sufficienter vitam tansigere non posset. Es igitur homini naturale, quod in societate multorum vivat. See *De Regimine Principium* in *Aquinas: Selected Political Writings*, edited by A.P. D'Entréves (Oxford: Basil Blackwell, 1948) p. 2, for the Latin text. The translation is from Aquinas, *On Kingship, to the King of Cyprus*, I, 1, in *Aquinas: On Law, Morality and Politics*, Edited by William p. Baumgarth and Richard J. Regan (Indianapolis: Hackett Publishing Company, 2nd Edition, 2002), 204.

[12] ordinat actus aliarum virtutum ad suum finem, quod est movere per imperium omnes alias virtutes. *S T* II-II 58, 6

[13] *ST* II-II 109, 3, ad 1 & 3.

Father T.C. O'Brien gives the helpful title "Virtues of Justice in the Human Community."[14]

OBEDIENCE AND THE ORDER OF JUSTICE IN GENERAL

As noted, Aquinas adopts the standard definition of justice from Roman law, "the constant and perpetual will to render to others what is their own."[15] From this fundamental statement about the virtue of justice an important question of social and political theory arises: are certain human beings owed obedience? Are other human beings obliged to obey? If so, what are the limits to authority and obedience, and who is the judge of those limits? Aquinas does not treat obligation per se, but rather the virtue of obedience. What follows is a discussion of the context of the question on obedience in the *Summa Theologiae,*[16] followed by an explanation of certain aspects of Aquinas' understanding of the virtue of obedience before turning to the more specific problem of civil obedience and the limits of civil authority.

The question on the virtue of obedience in the *Summa Theologiae* falls in a section of the *Summa* devoted to a variety of minor virtues connected to the virtue of justice.[17] Such virtues are said to share something in common with justice but fall short of the complete virtue. The list of virtues included in this category is derived in large part from Cicero's discussion of deliberative oratory in his juvenile treatise, *de Inventione*. In this account virtue is said to have four parts: prudence, justice, fortitude and temperance. In the passage on justice Cicero states that, "Natural right (*jus naturae*) is not born of opinion, but implanted in us by a kind of innate instinct: it includes religion,

[14] St. Thomas Aquinas, *Summa Theologiae*, Volume 41, "The Virtues of Justice in the Human Community" (Cambridge University Press, 2006 reprint).

[15] *ST* II-II, 58, 1, *Utrum convenienter definiatur justitia, quod est perpetua et constans voluntas jus suum unicuique tribuendi*. The immediate source of the definition is Ulpian's *Digest* 1, 1.

[16] *ST* II-II 104

[17] *ST* II-II 81-120

piety, gratitude, revenge, respect and truth."[18] The decision to rely on a work on rhetoric seems tied to the purpose of this section in the plan of the *Summa*, focused on virtues related to justice in human communities, and so, *conversatio*.[19] Our duties in our community arise from our relationships with others and therefore from an ongoing conversation.

Here we focus on the understanding of the acquired virtue of obedience in *Secunda Secundae*, question 104, "Of Obedience."[20] This is the third of three questions following from the virtue of respect (*observantia*). The first two questions deal with respect itself, and with or *dulia* (respectful service) respectively.[21] Respect is said to include honor or service to one's superiors as well as obedience to their commands. So the virtue of obedience, like respectful service, is reckoned to be part of respect. We will first consider the issue of obedience generally in terms of obedience to the command of God or of any human being or body of human beings who have some claim of superiority over some agent, and then turn to political or civil obedience and disobedience.[22]

Some preliminary observations about the way Aquinas approached the virtue of obedience are in order. Aquinas makes an important distinction having to do with the fact that acts of one virtue may be directed toward some objective that may pertain to another.[23] The example Aquinas uses is that of a soldier defending his king's stronghold. The soldier's actions exhibit both the virtue of obedience

[18] Cicero, *de Inventione* (II.52, 157ff).

[19] Cary Nederman has written extensively on the importance of the Ciceronian tradition in medieval political ideas and the way that it complicates the concept of "medieval Aristotelianism." See his "Nature, Sin and the Origins of Society: The Ciceronian Tradition in Medieval Political Thought," *Journal of the History of Ideas* 49 (1988) 3-26, "Aristotelianism and the Origins of 'Political Science' in the Twelfth Century," *Journal of the History of Ideas* 52 (1991) 179-194, and "The Meaning of Aristotelianism in Moral and Political Thought," *Journal of the History of Ideas* 57 (1996) 563-585.

[20] *ST* II-II, 104, *de obedientia.*

[21] *ST* II-II, 102 & 103.

[22] *ST* II-II 104, 1.

[23] *ST* II-II 104, 2.

and of courage. Similarly one might note that a citizen who obeys the command of the law by providing taxes exhibits both the virtue of obedience and of justice. A citizen who obeys a wise command from a legislator exhibits both the virtue of obedience and of prudence, and so on.

Another important consideration is that for Aquinas not all acts of obedience are virtuous, and that acts of obedience are virtuous in the same way. He discusses this in an intricate response to a point about the three vows of religious life: poverty, chastity and obedience. Once poverty and chastity are vowed, they are necessary for salvation as a matter of obligation, and are part of the way of life (*regular conversatio*) of the religious community. However, those in religious life may choose to obey in ways that are not commanded by their order, and are not forbidden by God or their order. He is here referring to various "counsels" that encourage Christians to super-ordinary virtue beyond what is necessary, by extensive fasting for instance or remaining in silence. In these cases, the virtue of obedience would be more perfect than that which is only obligatory. So we might say that there is obligatory obedience and perfect obedience.[24]

However, as noted, obedience is not always due to a human superior. According to Aquinas there is such a thing as indiscriminate obedience. So that there may be times when individuals must deliberate about a command and determine not to follow it. In order to summarize Aquinas' treatment of obedience and disobedience I will pose and respond to three questions: 1) Who are the superiors to whom one owes obedience? 2) Are there limits to the obedience one owes to human superiors? 3) What principles help us to establish the limits of virtuous, as opposed to indiscriminate obedience, and by extension the limits of various human authorities?

Aquinas held that obedience is owed to God simply. That is, one should obey all of the commands of God. According to John Courtney Murray this understanding is an important part of the traditional American consensus. It is reflected in the opening of the Declaration of Independence, which alludes to the "laws of nature and nature's" God, and consequently recognizes the sovereignty

[24] *ST* II-II 104, 4 ad 3.

of God over all nations and governments. This same view is acknowledged by Lincoln in his "Gettysburg Address." The United States is a nation "under God." From this Murray drew an important distinction between the understanding of human freedom and democracy characteristic of the United States and the secularizing Jacobin tradition of continental Europe.[25] According to Aquinas all human authority is by its nature limited, and related to some human purpose or purposes connected to the conditions of particular human communities. It is this view also that led Murray's contemporary Jacques Maritain to claim that the concept of political sovereignty is "intrinsically wrong and bound to mislead."[26] On this view even the absolute sovereignty of a democratic majority is a form of despotism.

Though they are "under God," human beings are left to their own counsel in the sense that they decide how to act based on their own faculties, and especially the faculty of practical reason.[27] Since God's commands are made known to us through natural law and divine revelation it is virtuous for one to offer loving obedience to God. This understanding of a person's free act of obedience to God leads us to the more immediate, but not unrelated question of obedience to the commands of other human beings. Like Aristotle, Aquinas conceives of society as having certain natural relations of ruling and subjection: parental rule over children, marital rule of husband over the wife, rule of the civil ruler over the subject.[28] Since

[25] Murray, *We Hold These Truths*, 44-46.

[26] See Maritain, *Man and the State* (University of Chicago Press, 1951) :"It is my contention that political philosophy must get rid of the word, as well as the concept, of Sovereignty…the concept is intrinsically wrong and bound to mislead us if we keep using it—…" 29. On the parallel careers of Murray and Maritain see John T. McGreevy, *Catholicism and American Freedom: A History* (New York: W.W. Norton & Company, 2003), Chapter Seven, "Democracy, Religious Freedom, and the Nouvelle Théologie," 189-215.

[27] *ST* II-II 104, 4.

[28] *ST* II-II 104, 5; Aquinas does not cite Aristotle's ordering of relations of rule and subjection in the household (*Politics* I, 1253^{a}ff) in these passages. On the political implications of Aquinas' understanding of natural equality and natural hierarchy see Mark C. Murphy, "Consent, Custom and the Common Good in Aquinas's Account of Political Authority," *Review of Politics* 59 (1997) 323-350.

this order is created by God, Aquinas views obedience to human authority as the normal course of action in the pursuit of the good.

In the question on obedience Aquinas does not mention the order of marital life as an issue having to do with the virtue of obedience. One might guess that this is because his work is in the first instance a type of recorded lecture for men in training to be priests, but it seems more likely that this reflects his interpretation of the contemporaneous understanding of marriage in canon law. In the law of the church marriage was understood to be a sacrament, both parties were understood to enter the covenant of their own free will, and both owed the same marriage debt (submission of their body to their spouse for the purpose of reproduction and the rearing of children).[29] This conception of marriage posits moral equality between spouses, even though theologians like Aquinas would have argued that the husband is naturally suited to head the household.

Besides these relations of the household and the civil association, there is also the religious order of the church based on charity.[30] In addition, in the 13th century, as today, there were a variety of social institutions and relationships in which people may have been bound to obey a superior in certain matters. For example the apprentice owes obedience to the master in a guild, the student to a teacher in a university, the soldier to a general, etc. Obedience in all of these relations would be limited to that specific objective for which each institution exists. One is obliged to obey the commands of superiors in societal institutions and relationships in order to accomplish that end for which the institution or relationship exists.[31] Therefore all authority relationships in human society are limited by the nature of the relationship and the purposes to which the relationship is

[29] See *ST Supplement to III,* 45. For an in depth study of the canon law of marriage during the middle ages see Charles J. Reid, *Power over the Body, Equality in the Family: Rights and Domestic Relations in Medieval Canon Law* (Grand Rapids: Eerdmans, 2004).

[30] *ST* II-II, 104, 5, ad 3.

[31] One might well argue that such relationships involve 'expertise' rather than authority, or that authority based on expertise is distinct from political authority. On these problems and others related to the concept of authority see Richard B. Friedman, "On the Concept of Authority in Political Philosophy," in Joseph Raz, editor, *Authority* (New York University Press, 1990) 56-91.

directed. In order to make clear the principles by which one may distinguish virtuous from indiscriminate obedience based on this view, it will be helpful to focus on the more specific problem of political or civil authority and obedience.

Aquinas believed that the subject is bound to obey the civil prince as part of the order of justice since without this obedience there could be no stability in society.[32] However his understanding of political rule must be understood in a medieval context. Aquinas, as mentioned above, held the then common view that human society is natural. It is necessary because human beings, unlike other animals, are not readily equipped with food, covering for protection from the climate and the means of self-defense. In addition human beings are naturally inclined to live in society and in conversation. So the civil ruler rules the many people in the society according to law for the common good.[33] Civil law becomes a rule and measure of the actions of individuals so that they may coordinate their individual actions with the common good. As Servais Pinckaers points out, law is viewed in this context as the work of wisdom rather than the constraint of freedom.[34]

Indiscriminate obedience entails one's obedience to a command that is unlawful with the understanding that commands may be unlawful in any number of ways and that one is not always duty bound to disobey unjust laws. As we shall see, the concept of indiscriminate obedience is particularly important to Aquinas' accounts of political obedience and disobedience. However, indiscriminate obedience could arise in any type of human relationship.

[32] This is explained in *Summa Theologiae* I, 96, 4, where Aquinas argues that even in the state of innocence human beings would have needed civil rule because many left to themselves are concerned with many things. Therefore civil rule is necessary to care for the common good, and people who live under civil government are still free human beings (*liberos*).

[33] See *ST* I, 96, 4; I-II, 105, 1 and *On Kingship* I, 1 & 6; and *ST* II-II, 47, 10 & 11 and 50, 1-2.

[34] *Morality: The Catholic View*, pp. 65-66.

LAW, OBEDIENCE AND PRUDENCE

According to Aquinas God must be obeyed in all things but a decision to obey a command of God rather than a command of the civil state is a deliberate act undertaken by a free subject. God's will is made known to human beings through commands, and the precepts of divine justice are summarized in the Decalogue, and perfected in the Great Commandments of the Gospel, to love God and to love one's neighbor as oneself.[35] Living according to order of charity is the highest form of virtue infused by divine grace.[36]

Given this it is not surprising that in the *sed contra* to article 5, Aquinas cites the statement that "…we ought to obey God rather than men," from the *Acts of the Apostles* (5, 29). His intention is to contrast the simple obedience that is due to God with the conditional obedience that subjects owe to their human superiors.[37] As T.C. O'Brien points out in an explanatory footnote,

> As a general principle St. Thomas maintains that no human superior has power over the inner life of other human beings.… Thus strictly speaking a human superior does not command the act of obedience, but the outward fulfillment of his command. The subject's obligation to render virtuous obedience in not to the superior precisely but to his own conscience, to the requirements of virtuous living, and so ultimately to God.[38]

In short, temporal authorities of all kinds, but especially civil legislators, command only outward physical acts. According to Aquinas civil laws that are just bind one in the forum of one's conscience. This was an uncharacteristic use of the term conscience as a synonym for practical reason, given that Aquinas explicitly defined conscience as an act of the practical intellect.[39] The decision to obey a command that is made in the form of one's conscience

[35] *ST* I-II, 100, 3 & II-II 122.

[36] *ST* II-II, 23, 6.

[37] *ST* II-II, 104, 5.

[38] *ST* II-II, 104, 5, fn. 10 at p. 68 in the Blackfriars edition.

[39] *ST* I-II 96, 4.

may be seen as an act of the virtue of prudence as well as the virtue of obedience. One chooses according to one's practical reason in a given set of circumstances, even and especially if one's practical reason determines that they not obey the command of the temporal superior. Consequently Aquinas held that prudence belongs to civil subjects to the extent that they must make decisions about the governance of their own affair.[40]

Notice that there is mode of learning implicit to this conception of the virtue of obedience as connected to the order of justice. Rightly willed acts of obedience over time lead to development of the virtue of prudence among the ruled, and potentially to all of the acquired virtues since they are connected through prudence. As we apprentice in our various walks of life we at first follow the model or command of our parents, teachers and other superiors. Over time we learn from them the reasons for which actions are undertaken through the experience of bringing them to completion and arriving at the desired purpose. Eventually we are able to understand how the actions we undertake are connected to purposes and can use this practical wisdom in similar applications. The Thomistic ethic places a strong emphasis on custom and habituation as necessary to the acquisition of virtue and liberty.[41]

Recently Professor Mary Keys has explained this in terms of what she calls Aquinas' "two pedagogies of law." Some contemporary scholars who focus on the doctrine of natural law in their interpretation of Aquinas's works have presented his understanding of human law in terms of the use of coercion and the threat of coercion to condition those who are viciously inclined. Professor Keys has argued that Aquinas held that the civil law also moves those who are already well-disposed to acquire virtue in a more complete and perfect sense. She calls this the positive pedagogy of the law, as opposed to the negative pedagogy stressed by Robert George and others.[42] Interestingly she, like Murray,

[40] *ST* II-II 47, 12.

[41] This point has been stressed in the works of Alasdair MacIntyre. See most recently *Ethics and Politics: Selected Essays, Volume 2* (Cambridge University Press, 2006) and *Dependent Rational Animals: Why Human Beings Need the Virtues* (Chicago: Open Court, 1999).

[42] Mary Keys, "Aquinas's Two Pedagogies: A Reconsideration of the Relation between

associates natural law with Lincoln's approach to law and government, citing his proclamation of an annual day of Thanksgiving.[43]

In the body of article 5 of question 104, Aquinas distinguishes three classes of human actions in which a person is not bound to obey the commands of their superior, and these are connected implicitly to the conception of natural inclinations to the good found in the *Treatise of Law* (I-II, 94, 2). The first class of actions involves circumstances in which one is not bound to obey the command of a human superior because of the command of a higher power, especially God. The second class of actions follows from the principle that human authority can only command the fulfillment of outward acts, and not the inner determination of the will according to practical reason. The third class of actions involves those things that pertain to the "nature" of the body (*ad naturam corporis pertinent*) and to which human beings have natural inclinations, since in these things all are equal. So that these are areas of human action in which each individual is at liberty even as a subject to a civil law.[44] The natural inclinations at issue in this third class of actions are those directed to bodily sustenance, procreation, and the education of the young. A hallmark example of Aquinas' determination to uphold human liberty in these areas of life can be found in his defense of the right of slaves to marry without the consent of their masters, even to the extent of requiring the master to allow the servant time to fulfill the marriage debt.[45]

Aquinas takes up the issue of political obedience in the final article of the question. By the time he commented on these issues in the *Secunda Secundae* he had thought through the duty of people who are subject to human law and had developed a view that requires the application of prudence by all members of a society who are subject to law. On the other hand Aquinas continued to uphold the apostolic endorsement of a moral obligation to obey civil rulers in order to

---

Law and Moral Virtue," *American Journal of Political Science*, 45 (2001) 519-531 and more recently her *Aquinas, Aristotle, and the Promise of the Common Good* (Cambridge University Press, 2006).

[43] Keys (2001) 528.

[44] *ST* II-II 104, 5.

[45] See *ST Supplement* to III, 51.

preserve the order of justice in political society.[46] The phrasing of the heading of the article, "Whether Christians must obey civil authority," implies some conflict between the commands of the civil ruler and the commands of God, and draws attention to St. Paul's treatment of that issue in Romans (13).

Our need for community is tied to bodily necessity and Aquinas contrasts human neediness with the situation of other animals that are readily supplied with the means of sustenance and defense. Nature drives people into life in political society to free human beings from natural necessity so that they can pursue the specifically human goods of moral and intellectual development.[47] The passages of *On Kingship* attributed to Aquinas contain an important statement about tyranny and resistance to tyranny. One passage deals with the classical question of the best regime.[48] Aquinas argues that it is best that rule in the human community be a kingship that mirrors divine providence which is rule by the one God. On the other hand the corruption of kingship yields the worst kind of government, tyranny. Yet tyranny arises more often from rule by the many than from kingship. Consequently Aquinas's argument for monarchy stresses that the person appointed to be king must be of the highest virtue, and that the people should take steps to insure that the king has no opportunity to become a tyrant.[49]

Aquinas never finished the portion of the work in which he might have discussed how kingship might be arranged to prevent tyranny, but he does develop a concept of the 'mixed regime' elsewhere.[50] In a discussion of the governing institutions of the ancient Israelites, he argues that a mixed regime of monarchy, aristocracy and democracy would be best:

[46] *ST* II-II 104, 6

[47] In *Aquinas; On Law, Morality, and Politics*, 204-206.

[48] *De regimine princupium* 1, 3 "That it is more beneficial for a community of men living together to be ruled by one than by many," in *Aquinas: Political Writings* (Cambridge University Press, 2002) 10ff.

[49] Ibid. 1,7at 17-18.

[50] *ST* I-II 105,1.

> ...it is a benign mixture of kingship, because there is one man who presides; of aristocracy, because it is the rule of several according to virtue; and of democracy, that is, popular power, because it belongs to the people to elect the rulers.[51]

It appears that the tendency in Aquinas' thought was to rely on customary arrangements to provide a constitutional monarchy, or republic that would prevent the rise of tyranny.[52]

When Aquinas took up the issue of resistance to tyranny in *On Kingship* he gave a number of practical reasons to tolerate tyranny if it is not "excessive." One might fail in an attempt to remove the tyrant leading to savage reprisals. If one were to succeed, the rebellion may sow the seeds of faction and future civil discord. Finally, if the people rely on the help of another ruler to overthrow the tyrant, that ruler may take over the tyranny and be even more oppressive than the other.[53] Aquinas then considers some heroic examples of resistance to tyranny in the Old Testament, but points out that these seem to contradict the Apostolic teaching of Peter, who teaches that one should obey even a master who is ill-disposed.[54] So, for Aquinas, it is the responsibility of those who hold some kind of public office to resist tyranny. Where it is the right of the community to provide a ruler for itself, it is also their right to depose a ruler. However, if some higher authority is given the right to appoint the king, the people should turn to him to depose the tyrant.[55]

[51] ibid.

[52] James Blythe has demonstrated that Ptolemy of Lucca's continuation of Aquinas's work seems to have significant influence on the development of republican ideas in the later Middle Ages and early modern periods. See Blythe, *Ideal Government and the Mixed Constitution in the Middle Ages* (Princeton: Princeton University Press, 1992) and Ptolemy of Lucca, *On the Government of Princes, with Portions attributed to Thomas Aquinas*, Translated by James M. Blythe (Philadelphia: University of Pennsylvania Press, 1997). Murray's understanding of republican government during the middle ages is derived from R.W. Carlyle and A.J. Carlyle, *A History of Medieval Political Theory in the West* (Edinburgh: William Blackwood and Son, 1903 and other dates). See Murray (2005, 298).

[53] *Political Writings*, at 18.

[54] Ibid. 19, citing 1 Peter 2:18f.

[55] Ibid. 20-21.

As noted above, there is a treatment of the issue of civil obedience and disobedience in the *Treatise of Law*. While Aquinas acknowledged that human law binds in conscience, if the law is just, in discussing the problem of unjust laws, Aquinas argued that they did not bind in conscience. The tone of this text is set by the *sed contra* which is taken from I Peter (2, 19), "This is grace that a person, for conscience sake, endure sorrows, suffering unjustly." However, there is no positing of a blanket duty to disobey unjust laws unless they command something directly contrary to the law of God (ex. idolatry).[56] Rather Aquinas suggests that one may obey unjust laws to avoid scandal or disturbances.[57]

Returning now to the article on political obedience and disobedience in the question on the virtue of obedience, the presentation is terse and focused.[58] The order of justice is strengthened, not abolished by faith in Christ. We are subject to other human beings as it regards the outward acts of our bodies, but our souls remain at liberty (*quae libera manet*).[59] Therefore we are obliged in conscience to obey the civil authorities, but this obligation must be measured according to the order of justice.[60] Thus we have no duty to obey a usurper or an unjust law, but we may do so because prudence dictates that we avoid scandal and public disorder.[61]

Aquinas made another statement about resistance to tyranny and unjust law in a question on sedition (II-II, 42). There he discussed the prudential issue of resistance to the tyrant in terms of the principle of the lesser evil, arguing that the tyrant should be removed unless the tumult that would result would cause the subjects to suffer more than the tyranny itself. There Aquinas openly states that tyranny is itself sedition, so that resistance to tyranny by the people is on the face of it justified.[62] This presents a view of society in which individuals

[56] On this point Aquinas' approach may differ from that of Dr. Martin Luther King's in his *Letter from the Birmingham Jail.*

[57] *ST I-II*, 96, 4,

[58] *ST* II-II, 104, 6.

[59] Ibid. as 1.

[60] Ibid, ad 3.

[61] Ibid.

[62] *ST* II-II 42, 2.

are formed to make prudent decisions about when to resist abuses of power and when not to resist. This prudence about political life and all acquired virtue could only arise through habituation in a civil community.

This type of prudence could not develop among people who were not part of an ongoing conversation, the living together and talking together of civil life in society. The type of apprenticeship each participant in this conversation experiences will differ depending on their individual pursuits. However, the point remains that we depend upon each other not just for bodily necessities, but also for the experiences that are necessary to develop virtue. By extension, the development of virtue, and especially the virtue of prudence, makes it possible for people to identify proximate goods (ends) and to formulate alternative plans of action.[63] Virtue, and most especially the virtue of prudence, is necessary for liberty to arise. Without the development of practical reason people are unable to fix on meaningful purposes and achieve their desired goals.

The idea that virtue is necessary for liberty is also part of John Courtney Murray's account of the American Consensus. Murray openly worried that this aspect of the consensus was threatened by the concept of "the conscience that knows no law higher than its own subjective imperatives" that had developed in the 19th century.[64] Later in his life when he commented on John Rawls' project of deontological liberalism he found it lacking. "Have we here another speculative effort to find in personal freedom the final root of moral obligations in and to society?" [65] If liberty does indeed arise from virtue, any attempt to derive social obligations from freedom must result in profound confusion.

Yet Murray argued that another part of the American consensus was that government was based on consent. How does one square this with an emphasis on natural law and virtue? Murray did not understand the principle of consent in the abstract terminology of contract theory, but

[63] I use the term "proximate ends" to stress that for Aquinas prudence deals only with means since he believed that the human end is the 'beatific vision.'

[64] Murray (2005) 50-51.

[65] "The Problem of Mr. Rawls' Problem," in *Law and Philosophy: A Symposium*, ed. by Sidney Hook (New York, 1964) p. 40, quoted in McGreevy (2003) 265.

rather in terms of the historical development of self-government from medieval times through the colonial period in the United States. The principle of consent was implicit in the medieval view of kingship and republicanism, and was developed in the colonies through their own experiences of self-government. Thus the American Consensus was based on a faith in the ability of the people to govern themselves that arose not from theory, but from the experience of a history of self-government.[66]

Consequently it may well be that the practice of enquiry that has developed out of Kantian approaches to ethics actually does more to confuse the narratives of our lives in society than it does to help us deliberate. An undue emphasis on the concepts of autonomy and obligation may impoverish our civil conversation since it should be focused on the identification of common purposes through conversation and deliberation.[67]

THE CIVIL CONVERSATION: LIBERTY FOR VIRTUE AND HAPPINESS

In the past two decades several trends in contemporary liberal democratic theory seem to be converging with Murray's concerns about the civil conversation. For the purposes of this essay I would like to draw attention to two examples of recent scholarship. Both examples offer versions of liberalism that treat autonomy and civic virtue as mutually reinforcing concepts rather than concepts that must be held in opposition. I am interested in the versions of liberalism promoted in recent works by Richard Dagger and William Galston where those authors discuss the kind of education necessary to encourage the virtues of a liberal polity.[68]

[66] Murray (2005) 48-50.

[67] Michael Sandel states this problem elegantly: "Since human beings are storytelling beings, we are bound to rebel against a drift to storylessness." See *Democracy Discontents: America in Search of a Public Philosophy* (Cambridge: Harvard University Press, 1996) p. 351.

[68] See Richard Dagger, *Civic Virtues: Rights, Citizenship, and Republican Liberalism* (Oxford University Press, 1997) and William Galston, *Liberal Purposes* (Cambridge Univer-

Both Dagger and Galston have proposed accounts of liberal democratic citizenship that move in the direction of Murray's argument in *We Hold These Truths*.[69] Murray noted that participation in the civil conversation that is the basis of liberal democracy required education and discipline of citizens' passions and prejudices. The accounts of liberalism constructed by Dagger and Galston also stress the importance to civic education in liberal democracy. There is a sense in which the accounts of civic education in these more recent works are actually more outdated than Murray's work, since they seem to remain wedded to an early modern and dualistic opposition of individualism and collectivism. Murray's approach to the American proposition attempts to be an approach for a society that is post-modern and post-Christian.[70]

One sign of this in the case of Galston's work is that his conception of civic education is explained almost exclusively in terms of formal education in public or private schools. After giving an account of liberal virtues that stresses the way they differ from classical virtue, he points out that there is no consensus on the empirical question of whether contemporary liberal society engenders the institutions and processes necessary for the habituation of such virtues.[71] Given this one would expect that Galston would have provided a more substantial account of the types of learning that he understands to be necessary

---

sity Press, 1991). Of course Dagger and Galston are only examples of a number of liberal theorists who have proposed perfectionist alternatives to the procedural liberalism advocated by scholars such as John Rawls and Ronald Dworkin. For further examples see Joseph Raz, *The Morality of Freedom* (Oxford: Clarendon Press, 1986), Stephen Macedo, *Liberal Virtues: Citizenship, Virtue, and Community in Constitutional Liberalism* (Oxford: Clarendon Press, 1990), George Sher, *Beyond Neutrality: Perfectionsim in Politics* (Cambridge University Press, 1997) and Peter Berkowitz, *Virtue and the Making of Modern Liberalism* (Princeton: Princeton University Press, 1999).

[69] It is also true that both authors are in part responding to critiques of contemporary liberalism raised by communitarian critics like Alasdair MacIntyre and Charles Taylor.

[70] On this point see Peter Augustine Lawler, "Murray's Natural-Law Articulation of the American Proposition," in Hunt & Grasso (1992) pp. 116-134. Murray (2005) states that "We know that the myopic individualism of modernity led it into other errors, even into the false conception of the problem of the state in terms of the unreal dichotomy, individualism vs. collectivism." (185).

[71] Galston (1992) 232-237.

for development of civic virtue in a liberal democracy. Instead his chapter on civic education remains entirely within the categories of formal school-based instruction. Within those categories Galston develops an account that provides more toleration for moral and religious traditionalism than the procedural liberalism his work seeks to correct, but there is no deeper consideration of the way that the inner light of human nature develops into virtue through observation and habituation.[72] This silence on the importance of informal education in the household and civil society is particularly striking given his detailed account of the empirical relationship between childhood poverty and broken families, a problem that is difficult to address through formal educational institutions.

Dagger's account of the development of autonomy and civic virtue in a liberal democracy is interesting in this regard. His 'republican liberalism' entails the belief that personal autonomy and civic virtue may be understood to be complementary. He understands autonomy as a human capacity to govern oneself, and argues that this capacity is social not only in its development but in its exercise.[73] Civic virtue is then explained in terms of a citizen's willingness to act with the common good in mind. This leads the argument into a consideration of the kind of communities that would encourage republican liberal citizenship.

The concept of a community applied by Dagger is borrowed from political scientist Michael Taylor, who conceives community as a matter of degree. Communities are said to have "shared values and beliefs, direct and many-sided relationships, and the practice of reciprocity."[74] Dagger argues that republican liberal citizenship can be explained in terms of the "assurance model," a game theoretic model derivative of Rousseau's stag hunt example. According to this model individual citizens will become 'conditional altruists,' rather than rational egoists of 'prisoner's dilemma,' because they have knowledge of the willingness of others to fulfill their duties to the community over a period of time. Dagger surmises that,

[72] Ibid. 241-289.

[73] Dagger (1997) p. 30-31, and 66-68.

[74] Taylor, *Community, Anarchy, and Liberty* (Cambridge: Cambridge University Press, 1982) p. 32, quoted in Dagger (1997) p. 112.

> The life of the active, public-spirited citizen is a demanding one, and under current conditions likely to be unrewarding as well. The person who plays the part of the republican-liberal citizen may also find that he or she is playing the part of the sucker, working futilely to help provide public goods while others try to enjoy these goods without bearing any of the costs of their production.[75]

One cannot help but to be puzzled by this hypothesis, given contemporary social scientific research that seems to demonstrate that active, publicly-spirited citizens tend to be more content than those who are not.[76] In order to compel those who would not be 'suckers' into their roles as citizens Dagger proposes an account of political obligation based on Rousseau's contract theory, thus attempting to ground a liberal account of citizenship with an account of the state that has profoundly illiberal implications.

When Dagger turns his attention to civic education he, like Galston, discusses the issue almost entirely in terms of the need for public schools that help to mold citizens for autonomy and civic virtue. These accounts reveal a clear assumption against educational choice, and especially against religious schools. Behind that assumption lies the view that religious education is likely to inhibit autonomy and the liberal virtues needed to encourage participation in the contemporary democracy. Here again, the two authors reason based on assumptions that are not clearly supported by empirical research. Sociologists Christian Smith and David Sikkink have studied the effects of private schools and home schooling on the levels of civic engagement among families in the United States. Controlling for a range of variables, they have concluded that private Catholic schools, other Christian schools, home school associations and nonreligious private schools embed their participants in networks that foster civic engagement better than do public schools.[77]

[75] Dagger, (1997) 109.

[76] See especially Robert Putnam's work on social capital, especially Putnam, with Roberto Leonardi and Raffaella Y. Nanetti, *Making Democracy Work: Civic Traditions in Modern Italy* (Princeton: Princeton University Press, 1993).

[77] Christian Smith and David Sikkink, "Is Private School Privatizing," *First Things* 92

Thus, while some contemporary liberal theorists concerned about virtue seem to be converging with Murray's account of the American consensus, these same theorists seem convinced that classical and Christian accounts of virtue are inconsistent with contemporary liberal democracy, and that political obligation must be justified based on contract theory or some similar intellectual device.

Here one must acknowledge the weaknesses of Murray's account as a basis for a contemporary consensus. Some time ago a sympathetic critic of Murray pointed out some key weaknesses in his attempt to expand the role of biblical discourse in the public life of the United States. One is that Murray's emphasis on liberty and limited government may appear to be a simple restatement of the liberal tradition that runs through Locke to contemporary libertarians like Robert Nozick. Another is that Murray failed to address the extent to which the natural law tradition rests upon specifically Catholic theological principles.[78] In virtually the same breath John Coleman pointed out that he shared Murray's pessimism about the potential for a revival of "classical republicanism." Be that as it may, republicanism, classical or otherwise, is exactly what is described by the language of the civil conversation and the American consensus that Murray urges upon us as we enter into the post-modern world.

If we shift our focus to the concept of conversation per se, it would seem that a good deal of convergence might be found between theorists of deliberative democracy and Murray's approach. However, though it is a burgeoning field of study, the deliberative theory of democracy is still ambiguous as it regards the opposition of individualism and collectivism. A recent approach defines deliberative democracy as:

(April, 1999) 16-20. On a related issue see Sikkink's "The Social Sources of Alienation from Public Schools," *Social Forces* 78 (1999) 51-86.

[78] John A. Coleman , "A Possible Role for Biblical Religion in Public Life," *Theological Studies* 40 (1979), reprinted in Charles E. Curran and Leslie Griffin (editors), *The Catholic Church, Morality and Politics* (New York: Paulist Press, 2001), 12-18.

> ... a form of government in which free and equal citizens (and their representatives), justify decisions in a process in which they give one another reasons that are mutually acceptable and generally accessible, with the aim of reaching conclusions that are binding in the present on all citizens but open to challenge in the future.[79]

Notice that here again the preoccupation of the authors is with the establishment of binding political obligations on autonomous individuals. What of their excellence and their happiness?

Just as Murray was becoming preoccupied with his work on the Second Vatican Council's declaration on religious freedom, he provided his interesting remarks in response to John Rawls' views on political obligation. He pointed out that his own approach to the problem derived from the Bible injunction of Romans 13 as interpreted through St. Augustine and scholasticism. The problem in this context is stated, "...how shall it be brought about, in theory and in practice, that in society man should, in the end, obey only God?"[80] This seems to close off Murray's ability to participate in much of the contemporary civil conversation as it was conceived by the late Professor Rawls and by deliberative democratic theory.

It may be that Murray's problem was his pessimism about the republican tradition and its potential to influence the civil conversation and the American proposition. The study of the language of republicanism and its plural significations is becoming an important part of contemporary studies in the history of political thought. The futility of the contemporary civil conversation may well give way to a new conversation, like that envisaged by the historian John McGreevy who writes that:

> Perhaps the final assessment of the long Catholic encounter with American ideas of freedom will rest here: on whether twenty-first-century Catholics can convince their fellow citizens, and themselves that associations and

[79] See Amy Gutman and Dennis Thompson, *Why Deliberative Democracy* (Princeton: Princeton University Press, 2004) p. 7.

[80] See Murray (1963) p.32.

> ties with the strangers in our midst satisfy our deepest, and most common aspirations.[81]

Here a contemporary historian of the experience of Catholics in the United States draws our attention back to the medieval republican view of a civil conversation discussed throughout this essay. Catholics who would seek associations with others could do worse than to adopt the understanding of the value of civil life one finds in Aquinas, and that is transformed into a contemporary discourse about human dignity in the "Declaration of Religious Freedom" (*Dignitatis Humanae*). With that said, it should be noted that the medieval republican discourse in which Aquinas was a participant includes a broad and elaborate set of problems and arguments that may provide us resources for our understanding of contemporary life. An exclusive focus on Aquinas and the language of natural law is no longer a logical strategy for a Catholic participant in the contemporary civil conversation of the United States.

[81] See McGreevy (2003) p.295.

THE NATURAL LAW IN THE MINDS OF THE FOUNDING FATHERS

William. C. Plouffe, Jr.

INTRODUCTION

The Founding Fathers of the United States of America, who launched the American Revolution and penned the Declaration of Independence, the Constitution, and the Bill of Rights, have been both deified and vilified, depending upon what view that faction is attempting to support or criticize and what position is attributed to the Founding Fathers. This has resulted in a continuing argument as to what the Founding Fathers were actually trying to say when they wrote these documents. The question of original intent plagues not only scholars in their pursuit of understanding but also the United States Supreme Court in its decision making to this day.

Two important schools of thought concerning this issue are: 1) original intent—which holds the position that the original intent of the Founding Fathers should be the guiding principle for the interpretation and application of these documents, and 2) living document—which holds that these documents should be considered to be living growing documents and are interpreted and applied according to the changing societal, political and legal values of the nation.[1] Thus, both the philosophical understanding and the legal application of these documents depend upon what these documents actually mean and how they are to be applied.

One of the most important questions as to the understanding and application of these documents is the existence, definition, extent, and/or limits to "rights"—be they human rights, civil rights, political rights, or natural rights. This is so because throughout these documents are references to and reservations of various rights to the individual person. However, interpretation of these references has created controversies that have even resulted in bloodshed, as shown by the Civil War, the labor movement during the late 1800s and early 1900s, and the civil rights movement of the 1950s and 1960s.[2]

[1] Jack N. Rakove, *Original Meanings: Politics and Ideas in the Making of the Constitution*, 3-22, 339-65 (Knopf 1997).

[2] Howard Zinn, *A People's History of the United States* (rev. ed., Harper 1995).

The question of rights, independent of statutory grants, has generally been referenced as the study of "natural rights" or "natural law." The essential reason for this classification is that the source of these rights is considered to be supra-positive, that is, beyond the positive (i.e., the written, established, or enacted) law based in nature itself—whether nature is the physical or non-physical universe. There is no argument that rights can originate in positive law. Indeed, some "rights" do have their originating basis in positive law. However, most rights granted by positive law generally have some basis in the natural law recognition of certain underlying values.

The Founding Fathers, for men of their day, were, for the most part, highly educated and well-read individuals. They had classical educations. Thus, it logically follows that what they read and under what doctrines and theories they were educated very well may have had a profound effect on their views. Indeed, many works indicate that the Founding Fathers were influenced by particular philosophers and scholars.[3]

Original intent on the part of the Founding Fathers is, arguably, an important, if not the fundamental, element of the legal and philosophical interpretation of the Declaration of Independence, the Constitution, and the Bill of Rights. The focus of this article will be an examination of these works of the Founding Fathers and a determination of whether natural law had any effect upon the Founding Fathers and their seminal works. Of course, this endeavor will attempt to determine what type of natural law the Founding Fathers employed, assuming natural law is found to be present in their work.

A BRIEF HISTORY OF THE NATURAL LAW TO THE TIME OF THE FOUNDING FATHERS

Prologue

Natural law has been defined in a number of ways. Essentially, it has been approached from four distinct perspectives: 1) as a function of physical natural laws, 2) as dependent upon theological

[3] See generally Carl J. Richard, *The Founders and the Classics* (Harvard 1994).

mandates, 3) as originating in a non-physical realm independent of theistic considerations, or 4) as a result of reason and rational determination.

The physical laws of nature are, by definition, natural laws. These natural laws are not the focus of this thesis, which is concerned with natural law as a guide or code for human social, political, and legal behavior. I recognize that in a physically deterministic world, any discussion of natural law would, by necessity, be limited to this approach to natural law. However, an assumption of this work is free-will. Thus, this perspective on natural law, as a function of mechanical or physical determinism, will not be considered.

A common approach to understanding natural law has been from the theological perspective. Under this approach, the source of natural law is, essentially, the will of a divine entity or agency. In contrast to mundane positive law (i.e., the written law), theological natural law is not something which is created or enacted by human agencies. The values, and hence the "rights" of each individual person, which underlie theological natural law are dependent upon each particular religion's mores and usually not subject to individual choice. Such values or "rights" are generally considered divinely inspired or mandated.

A third approach to understanding natural law has been the seeking of it in the non-physical but non-theistic realm of existence. Of course, this position assumes the existence of such a "spiritual" or non-material realm, for which there is no theological or divine influence. This approach overlaps with the theological approach (in that it implies some sense of naturalistic divinity) and with the rational approach to determining natural law (in that, generally, the rational faculty must be employed to understand the natural law).

The last approach to understanding natural law has frequently been labeled the rational approach. This method requires the use of the rational faculty (i.e., the mind) to determine and understand what the principles of natural law are or should be. The results of this approach are dependent upon what underlying values are either selected or acknowledged by the entity stating or expressing the principles of natural law. The underlying values, whether explicit or implicit, will form the foundation for what is considered to be the natural law. Under this theory of natural law, there has been much debate if the expressed principles are actually natural law, especially when the underlying values are challenged, as opposed to mere choices.

Essentially, these four perspectives of natural law encompass two views of the ontological nature of natural law. The first view is that natural law has a separate independent existence, that is, the existence of natural law is not dependent upon any perception, acknowledgment, or creation of the natural law by a human being or any other entity for its existence. The natural law has its own separate existence in the universe. This ontological view of the natural law is associated with the first and third perspectives of natural law explained above.

The first ontological perspective is easily understood as, essentially, the natural law could be likened to an expression of the relationships between the various elements of the physical universe. Thus, it has a separate existence from the human beings who perceive it. The third perspective acknowledges the natural law as originating in a non-physical, non-theistic realm. In this sense, the natural law is more of a principle that has a separate existence from human beings than as a maxim of behavior mandated by a divine entity or human being. A prime example of this perspective is Immanuel Kant, even though his philosophy of natural law was not developed or well-known until after the period of the American revolution. Essentially, Kant expressed this existence of natural law as a separation of law from morality, where morality was internal to each human being and law was external.[4]

The second ontological perspective of the natural law is as a creation of a divine entity or the human beings who apply it. This perspective includes the second and fourth views expressed above. Essentially, under this perspective, the natural law exists because either the divine entity mandates it or human beings create it as a rational extension of certain moral values. These values are only valid with respect to human beings and have no intrinsic value outside the perspective of human beings. Thus, natural law is dependent for its existence on human beings.

[4] Heinrich A. Rommen, *The Natural Law, A Study in Legal and Social History and Philosophy* 88-89 (Liberty Fund 1998).

To provide a coherent background of natural law thought up to the time of the Founding Fathers, I will provide a chronological presentation of the major natural law philosophers. Hopefully, this will provide the reader with an understanding of the philosophical influences upon the Founding Fathers at the time they wrote the Declaration of Independence, the Constitution, and the Bill of Rights.

The Pre-Socratic Philosophers

The first western philosophers are known for their attempts to understand nature by the identification of a single fundamental element that comprised the universe. For example, Thales thought it was water, Anaximenes thought it was air, and Heraclitus thought it was fire. These philosophers implicitly recognized that there was a single universal principle to the physical operation of the universe, but apparently did not apply their theories of natural law to the political or legal fields.

Plato

Plato is the first major natural law philosopher in western thought. Using Socrates as a primary character, Plato presented Socratic/Platonic philosophy in the *Dialogues*.

The first harbinger of natural law in the Dialogues is found in the *Charmides*.[5] In the *Charmides*, Socrates attempted to determine what compromises the ultimate ideal of "sophrosyne." Essentially, the ideal of sophrosyne encompassed a form of temperance, which implied the existence of natural laws which included harmony and proportionality.[6] Plato clearly held the position, even if not explicitly stated, that following the natural order of the universe was natural law,[7] as so clearly shown in the *Republic*. Indeed, civil society was not possible without adherence to the natural law.[8]

[5] *Charmides* in *Plato, The Collected Dialogues* (Edith Hamilton & Huntington Cairns, eds., Princeton 1963).

[6] *Charmides*, 157d, 159b-d, 160b, 162, & 167.

[7] *Gorgias*, 499e-500b & 526d-527; *Republic*, 456b-c, 484c-d, 500d, & 501b; *Laws*, 794d-795d.

[8] *Republic*, 423a-c; *Laws*, 681c-d, 708b-d, & 738d-e.

The natural order for Plato encompassed the non-material realm of the ideal, where each item, quality, or principle had an ideal form. This ideal form existed only in the non-material world and each form was the perfect expression of what was observed or perceived in the material world.[9] This same conception of form applied to such principles as justice and law as it did to material objects.

The ideal state, for Plato, would include no positive laws, as such laws have always resulted in abuse or a ruler who failed to follow the natural order.[10] In the ideal state, a statesman (more commonly known as the philosopher-king), and not a traditional hereditary king, committed to wisdom and the natural order and able to perceive truth, beauty, and justice would have supreme power and not be subjected to written laws which could be manipulated to serve unscrupulous men.[11] However, that statesman would, ideally, be subject to the natural law—which is the absolute form of truth and justice.Thus, for Plato, natural law was the requirement that a person should follow the natural order of the universe, personified in the ideal world of forms. For any given social, political, or legal circumstances, there was a just way to act. Unfortunately, in the *Dialogues*, no answer was ever really given to defining what constituted perfect justice,[12] although reflections of justice could be seen in the *Dialogues* in the discussions of what was not just. In the *Republic*, there was discussion as to what general qualities were needed for certain roles in society (i.e., courage for the soldiers and wisdom for the philosopher-kings), but the only reflections on what was ultimate justice was that each should be given "their due." Unfortunately, what was "their due" was defined by positive law, which was often faulty.

Under this theory of natural law, it was recognized that all men were not created equal, as each had differing needs and qualities.[13] Interestingly, this contradicts common modern notions of natural law, which generally holds that all people are created equal and have equal rights.

[9] *Phaedo*; *Republic*, Book VI; *Parmenides*, 127-135.

[10] *Laws*, Book III; *Statesman*, 301b-d.

[11] *Statesman*, 308-309e; *Republic*, 484-485.

[12] *Republic*.

[13] *Republic*, 374e-376c, 485a-487a.

In the context of the categories of natural law previously presented, Platonic natural law would fall within the non-theistic, non-material type of natural law. Although little guidance as to what specific actual principles of justice or natural law were provided, Plato is important as being one of the first to recognize that there existed a non-material, non-positive law upon which behavior should be based. However, there is a significant element of reason to Plato's theory of natural law, as it is through reason that the natural law is perceived and acknowledged.

Aristotle

Aristotle, Plato's student, developed a philosophy that was different from his teacher that was based on the material world rather than the realm of forms. It must be remembered that neither Aristotle nor Plato ever expressed any complete and coherent theory of natural law. Their positions on natural law are formulated from various unconnected references in different works.[14] In the *Politics*, Aristotle presented his famous statement that man is a political animal and acknowledged that man arose from a state of nature.[15] Based, in part, on this statement, Aristotle has been occasionally referred to as the father of natural law theory. Indeed, in the *Nicomachean Ethics*, Aristotle acknowledged the existence of a natural law.[16] Aristotle equated adherence to excellence in accordance with a rational principle as the ultimate good.[17] Aristotle went on to acknowledge that political justice (i.e., natural law) exists and has the same applicability to all people, regardless of what people think.[18]

Simply stated, this is a restatement of the Platonic principle that adherence to the natural order or the natural law was the ultimate good. Aristotle, like Plato, also recognized that a civil society was

[14] Brian Bix, *Natural Law Theory* in *A Companion to Philosophy of Law and Legal Theory* 223-24 (Dennis Patterson, ed., Blackwell 1996).

[15] *Politics*, 1253a, in *II The Complete Works of Aristotle* (Jonathan Barnes, ed., Princeton 1984).

[16] Nichomachean Ethics in II The Complete Works of Aristotle (Jonathan Barnes, ed., Princeton 1984).

[17] *Nichomachean Ethics,* 1098a.

[18] *Nichomachean Ethics*, 1134b.

simply not possible unless it was organized in accord with the natural order.[19]

Also like Plato, Aristotle recognized that not all men were equal, each differed according to their abilities and qualities.[20] Accordingly, Aristotle held the position that, in accordance with natural law, each person should accept the position in society for which they were suited. However, also like Plato, Aristotle was remarkably lacking in defining the absolute principles of natural law (except for general references to certain qualities required to accomplish political tasks), which should guide the selection process and who should make the selections, even though Aristotle recognized that it was nature that defined justice.[21] Nonetheless, whatever justice might be, it was universal and binding on all men.[22] Like Plato, Aristotle did not provide a comprehensive definition of justice.

Unlike Plato, Aristotle provided extensive descriptive works that described the physical nature of the universe. These works included, *inter alia*, the *Physics*, the *Metaphysics*, and numerous works on biology. For the most part, these works addressed the physical laws of the universe but did not specifically address the application of natural law to the social, political, or legal questions that have been usually associated with the study of natural law. Aristotle approached the study of nature in an empirical manner.

Aristotle then attempted to apply this empiricism to the study of humanity. Doing so, Aristotle arrived at the conclusion that humanity was superior to the other animals by the possession of reason.[23] However, even though Aristotle acknowledged that reason could be faulty, it was the perfection of reason that was the highest goal of nature.[24] Indeed, the ultimate human good was the exercise

[19] *Nichomachean Ethics*, 1170b-1171a; *Politics*, 1253a.

[20] *Nichomachean Ethics*, 1095b, 1179b-1180a; *Politics*, 1254a, 1267b, 1327b.

[21] *Nichomachean Ethics*, 1135a.

[22] Yves R. Simon, *The Traditions of Natural Law* 131 (Vikan Kuic, ed., Fordham 1965).

[23] *Politics*, 1332b.

[24] *Politics*, 1334b.

of both practical and theoretical rationality.[25] From this premise, for Aristotle, natural law was living in accord with the principle of excellence for the ultimate good. Although Aristotle did not specifically define the ultimate good (indeed, he acknowledged it could be different for each person[26]), he acknowledged that the good life involved acting in moderation and in proportion to the circumstances presented.[27]

However, even though Aristotle recognized that the natural law existed and applied to all people, it did not follow that the natural law existed in a non-material plane, such as was the case for Platonic philosophy. Aristotle recognized that there was a soul, but that soul was inextricably part of the material body.[28] As the material world was the essential plane of existence for Aristotle, the natural law did not originate in a non-material world but was only recognized by the rational faculty of humankind. Thus, Aristotelian natural law falls within the category of natural law of rational determination of the natural law as a physical manifestation of the natural order of the physical universe or rational acknowledgment of that natural order.

Cicero (106-43 B.C.)

The Roman world made a significant contribution to the development of natural law theory in the civilized world. The Romans formalized the distinction between the natural law and the civil law, and recognized that the civil law must yield to the natural law when the two conflict.[29] Indeed, it was Justinian who first codified the conceptions of law as: the natural law which was the set of general principles applicable to all, the law of nations which was the natural law as applied to nations as there was no codified

[25] C.C.W. Tayler, *Politics* in *The Cambridge Companion to Aristotle* 234 (Jonathan Barnes, ed., Cambridge 1995).

[26] *Politics,* 1260b25.

[27] *Nichomachean Ethics,* 1100a-1101b.

[28] *On the Soul* in *I The Complete Works of Aristotle* (Jonathan Barnes, ed., Princeton 1984).

[29] Heinrich A. Rommen, *The Natural Law, A Study in Legal and Social History and Philosophy* 25 (Liberty Fund 1998).

law between nations, and the civil law which was the codified law for citizens in a political community.[30]

The Stoic school of thought in the Roman world was one of the most influential in the field of natural law in the ancient world.[31] The Stoics were renowned for stressing the universality of natural law, such that it applied to all persons and not just particular groups of people.[32] Indeed, the basis of the Roman system of law was that the civil law was meant to be an expression of the natural law, such that even a judge was not the source of the law but was also subject to the law.

One of the greatest spokesmen for Roman jurisprudence was the Stoic philosopher, Cicero. On the topic of natural law, Cicero advanced the principle that nature is the ultimate authority of what is just.[33] For example, this included the obligation to help others.[34] What is just, in accordance with the natural law, is dependent upon right reason and not the edicts of mere men, as men can and do enact laws which permit injustice.[35] Thus, Cicero's vision of what was right under the natural law was dependent upon certain principles of equity. Such acts as theft and murder would be transgressions of the natural law.

Under this principle, people were morally obligated to follow the natural order, which amounted to natural law.[36] Cicero's vision of the natural law, like Plato and Aristotle before him, did not acknowledge the ultimate equality of all people. For Cicero, differences under the law for different people, depending upon their qualities and positions, were acceptable.[37]

[30] Carl Joachim Friedrich, *The Philosophy of Law in Historical Perspective* 25 (Chicago 1963).

[31] Brian Bix, *Natural Law Theory* in *A Companion to Philosophy of Law and Legal Theory 224 (Dennis Patterson, ed., Blackwell 1996).*

[32] Yves Simon, *The Tradition of Natural Law* 30-31 (Vikan Kuic, ed., Fordham 1965).

[33] Cicero, *Laws*, ii, 13 & 40; *De Finibus*, iv, 72, v. 17.

[34] Rosina L. Hunt, *Natural Law vs. Positive Law: Interpreting Morality*, 28 New. Eng. L. Rev. 231, 248-49 (1933).

[35] Cicero, *Laws,* xvi.

[36] Cicero, *Laws*, i, 17, 25-27, 45, & 58-73; *De Finibus*, ii, 33-34, iv, 16, 25, 34-37, v. 26.

[37] Cicero, *Laws*, i, 28-35; *De Finibus*, iv, 21; *Republic*, iii, 4, 37-38.

According to Cicero and the Stoic view, natural law was an unchanging standard by which to measure justice.[38] Recognition of what was just under the natural law was dependent upon reason, which was a function of nature, but the natural law did not exist because of reason.[39] Thus, Cicero and the Stoics fall within that type of natural law that depends upon rational determination for an understanding of what is just.

Saint Thomas Aquinas (1225-1274)

Aquinas is, without a doubt, the most famous proponent of natural law in western thought.[40] Further, he is probably the first natural law philosopher to present a relatively comprehensive explanation of natural law and its application.

Aquinas presented an initial definition of law in his seminal work, the *Summa Theologica.* Law, according to Aquinas, is a compelling force that governs behavior according to a certain standard based on reason for the common good.[41] To be a valid law, it had to be promulgated by a legitimate sovereign. If a law violated reason, it was not valid.[42]

Aquinas identified four separate types of law: eternal law, natural law, human law, and divine law, but he acknowledged that they were all related in some form. Eternal law was that law which represented the unknowable reason/will of God.[43] The only way humankind could become aware of eternal law was through its effects.[44]

[38] Brian Bix, *Natural Law Theory in A Companion to Philosophy of Law and Legal Theory* 224 (Dennis Patterson, ed., Blackwell 1996).

[39] Carl Joachim Friedrich, *The Philosophy of Law in Historical Perspective* 30 (Chicago 1963).

[40] Brian Bix, "Natural Law Theory" in *A Companion to Philosophy of Law and Legal Theory* 225 (Dennis Patterson, ed., Blackwell 1996).

[41] Thomas Aquinas, *Summa Theologica*, Q.90-A.1, Q.90-A.4.

[42] *Summa Theologica*, Q.90-A.4.

[43] *Summa Theologica*, Q.91-A.3.

[44] *Summa Theologica*, Q.93-A.1 & -A.2.

Natural law, for Aquinas, was the imprint of the eternal law on the consciousness of each person.[45] Natural law existed for all forms of life, but it was different for humankind in comparison to the animals of the world.[46] The basis for this difference was due to the presence of reason in each human being. Natural law had two basic aspects: 1) natural qualities which were related to physical properties, and 2) natural inclinations which were related to behavior linked to desires such as sex and drink.[47] Natural law for humans included the following mandates or qualities: 1) good is to be done and evil is to be avoided, 2) the right to self-preservation, 3) natural inclinations given to humankind, such as sex, and 4) reason is good and should be used to know God and gain knowledge.[48] Aquinas recognized a third aspect applicable to natural law but not encompassed within the natural law, which was a moral obligation placed on each person to act in a good manner as a dictate of reason.[49] This moral obligation highlighted how reason and will had an important role to play in Aquinas' theory of natural law.

Because the natural law was an imprint on each human being of the eternal law, it was different for all people and changeable. The natural law (i.e., the imprint of the eternal law on each human being) could be corrupted by adverse experiences, passions, and evil.[50] Thus, in contrast to the natural law philosophy of Plato, Aristotle, and Cicero, the natural law of Aquinas was not an unchanging set of moral principles but, rather, an incomplete reflection of a higher law. Essentially, Aquinas' natural law was merely a partial expression of the eternal law.

In actuality, the eternal law of Aquinas is probably a more accurate reflection of what Plato, Aristotle, and Cicero considered to be natural law. Aquinas' eternal law seems to have all the same qualities as the natural law of the ancient philosophers, such as,

[45] *Summa Theologica*, Q.91-A.2

[46] *Summa Theologica*, Q.91-A.6.

[47] *Summa Theologica*, Q.94-A.3.

[48] *Summa Theologica*, Q.92-A.4.

[49] *Summa Theologica*, Q.94-A.3.

[50] *Summa Theologica*, Q.94-A.5.

for example, the unknowable aspects of both laws. The difference between Aquinas and the ancient philosophers can be considered to merely be one of labeling and semantics.

Human law was that law, according to Aquinas, that was created to address those particular and specific situations which were not addressed by either the eternal law or the natural law.[51] Aquinas noted that human law was especially needed as only humans, of all the animals, have the ability to pervert their natural inclinations as human reason and will are weak, which allows them to stray from the natural law.[52] This possibility of change in the natural law highlighted the importance of reason in Aquinas' theory of natural law. Any person could exercise his reason and will and overcome adverse experiences, obstacles, and evil. By doing so, a person could approach the ultimate good, but it depended upon the exercise of reason and will.

Aquinas was somewhat ambivalent about the definition of divine law. At one point he equated it with eternal law, but then qualified his definition by stating that divine law was the pure expression of eternal law in terms that were comprehensible to human beings.[53] An example would be the Ten Commandments.

For Aquinas, the purpose of all law, to include the natural law, was the ultimate good.[54] Aquinas, as a Catholic theologian, presented the divine good as happiness in life, for which the ultimate end was God. This ultimate good under Aquinas' theory of natural law focuses more on the end, which is God, as opposed to the theories of natural law advanced by the ancient philosophers which have a much stronger focus on truth and knowledge, combined with reason, as the vehicle for realization of the natural law.

Aquinas' theory of natural law, then, clearly falls within that type of natural law which focuses on theological mandates. What is the natural law for Aquinas is merely a partial expression of the divine will. Although reason has a place, it is not nearly as important as it is for the ancient philosophers. However, Aquinas' theory of

[51] *Summa Theologica*, Q.91-A.3.

[52] *Summa Theologica*, Q.95-A.1.

[53] *Summa Theologica*, Q.91-A.4.

[54] *Summa Theologica*, Q.90-A.2.

natural law can, arguably, stand on its own without dependence on theological mandates.

King James I (1566-1625)

Throughout history until the time of the Founding Fathers, one of the more common forms of government was the monarchy. One of the essential features of a monarchy was the transfer of power through hereditary succession. However, under a theory of natural law applied to monarchies, succession was deemed by some to be a divine right. The theory was most aptly expressed by King James I of England, in his work *The True Law of Free Monarchies*.[55]

King James essentially relied on the Bible to establish that the monarchy was a divine institution. Further, he noted that the first oath of a monarch on his coronation was to enforce the divine law. Thus, the monarch's subjects had a duty to obey the king. However, King James was not content to rely on just theological authority. He also invoked natural law. By virtue of the monarch's position over his subjects, he became a natural father to his subjects and, thus, had the same authority over his subjects as a father had over his children. The monarch was bound to care for his subjects but his subjects were bound to obey him.[56]

Accordingly, the natural law theory of divine right to political power, as expressed by King James, falls within that type of natural law that depends upon theological mandate.

Hugo Grotius (1583-1645)

Hugo Grotius was a Dutch philosopher of great importance in the development of both natural law and international law. Grotius attempted to develop a coherent theory of international law that rested on principles of natural law and positive law. Grotius' major

[55] King James I, *The True Law of Free Monarchies* in *I The Great Political Theories* 313 (Michael Curtis, ed., Avon 1981).

[56] King James I, *The True Law of Free Monarchies* in *I The Great Political Theories* 314-15 (Michael Curtis, ed., Avon 1981).

work was *The Law of War and Peace*. On this work, much of the work of future generations of philosophers and legal scholars has rested.

Grotius held the position that the law of nature was a dictate of right reason, which had to be in conformity with rational and social nature.[57] What was unjust was that which was repugnant to the nature of a society of reasonable creatures.[58] Under the natural law, each man was obligated to do that which was moral and commendable.[59] Essentially, human nature had two aspects: 1) the physical human drives combined with the instinct of self-preservation and 2) the ability of right reason.[60] Thus, under the natural law, each person had the right of: 1) power over themselves, 2) owning property, and 3) demanding what was due to them and rendering what was due to others.[61] Although each person did not have the right to harm another, under the power over themselves, each person had the right to defend themselves.

Grotius was a leader of his time based on his statement that was, for the time period, controversial, to say the least. Even though much of the previous natural law theory of the time rested on religious values, Grotius claimed that the natural law would exist even if God did not exist.[62] What this statement did was begin the process of change in natural law philosophy from a religious-based theory to a secular theory.[63] Grotius also subscribed to the universal application of the natural law.

Accordingly, Grotius' theory of natural law clearly falls within that type of natural law that depends upon rational determination, despite his many references to religion in his description and analysis.

[57] Hugo Grotius, *The Law of War and Peace,* Book I, 1.

[58] *The Law of War and Peace*, Book I, 1, iii-iv.

[59] *The Law of War and Peace*, Book I, 1, ix.

[60] *The Law of War and Peace*, Book I, 2, i.

[61] *The Law of War and Peace*, Book I, 1, v.

[62] *The Law of War and Peace*, Prolegomena, XI-XII.

[63] Carl Joachim Friedrich, *The Philosophy of Law in Historical Perspective* 65 (Chicago 1963).

Thomas Hobbes (1588-1679)

Thomas Hobbes, a seventeenth-century philosopher, was renowned for his rather bleak view of the human condition and nature. His views were expressed in his work *Leviathan*.[64]

Hobbes recognized that the natural condition of human beings was one of war, where each was vying with the other for the necessities of life. Essentially all men were equal, despite minor differences of strength or intelligence; each man had the liberty, as a right of nature, to take whatever he wanted from another man.[65] This state of nature, for Hobbes, was a dismal affair from the overall perspective of humanity, where each man's self-interest was the only value: "And the life of man, solitary, poore, nasty, brutish, and short."

Accordingly, Hobbes posited the existence of an overriding law of nature that man should not do anything destructive of his life or destructive of the means for preserving his life.[66] The basis for this law was the self-interest of humanity—self preservation, thus, it was universally applicable to all men. This "natural law" was not based on any higher good, as the phrase is commonly used by philosophers, but on the basis of self-interest.[67] In support of this overall law of nature, Hobbes presented a number of subordinate laws of nature to actualize the preservation of each man.

Of these subordinate laws of nature, the first three were the most important from a political perspective. The first law of nature was that each man ought to work for peace whenever possible, otherwise, he ought to fight a war using all means at his disposal. The second law of nature was that each man should, where other men are willing to do the same, surrender his right to all things and surrender some portion of his liberty to ensure the peace.[68] The third law of nature was that men should keep their agreements, otherwise peace would

[64] Thomas Hobbes, *Leviathan* (Everyman's Library 1979).
[65] *Leviathan*, XIV, 63-67.
[66] *Leviathan*, XIV, 66.
[67] Carl Joachim Friedrich, *The Philosophy of Law in Historical Perspective* 85 (Chicago 1963).
[68] *Leviathan*, XIV, 67.

never occur.[69] These three subordinate laws of nature, if employed, would tend to allow the primary law of nature to have effect for all men, and not just the strongest. Even though actualization of these three subordinate laws of nature would defeat each man's natural right to all things, it would maximize the law of nature of self-preservation for all men.

Hobbes also presented a number of other subordinate laws of nature that addressed other aspects of keeping the peace, but these laws were more geared towards interpersonal relationships rather than broad questions of political or legal philosophy.[70] However, one of them did present a principle worth noting. Hobbes' eleventh law of nature mandated the application of the principle of equity in dealings between men.[71] By his acknowledgment of this principle, Hobbes implicitly recognized that all men deserved equal treatment under the law, in reflection of the equality they had in the state of nature, and that such equal treatment was a necessary requirement under the natural law.

It is interesting to compare Hobbes' view of human equality to that of the ancient philosophers. Where the ancient philosophers appeared not to recognize the inherent philosophical equality of all people, despite differences of ability, Hobbes did so. In this sense, Hobbes foreshadowed the development of the concept of equal protection of the law, which is a principle enshrined in the Constitution and the Bill of Rights.

Hobbes averred that these natural laws were immutable and eternal and their application was based on reason. However, Hobbes did recognize that even though the natural law was a result of the dictates of reason, it was delivered in the word of God.[72] Indeed, in his discussion of the second law of nature, Hobbes specifically referred to the Gospel and the Golden Rule of doing unto others as you would have them do unto you.[73]

[69] *Leviathan*, XV, 74.
[70] *Leviathan*, XV, 78-81
[71] *Leviathan*, XV, 80.
[72] *Leviathan*, XV, 82-83.
[73] *Leviathan*, XIV, 67.

It must be realized that, for Hobbes, according to some commentators, the natural law could not be used to justify revolt against the positive law which had been enacted.[74] This conclusion appears to contradict Hobbes' basic principle that each human has the natural right to take what he wants.

Accordingly, Hobbes' theory of natural law falls within that theory of natural law that is determined by reason. Hobbes' refusal to acknowledge any underlying values of a higher good to his theory of natural law has prompted the criticism that it is not really a theory of natural law.[75] Despite his references to the word of God, Hobbes' acknowledged that it merely delivered the natural law, it did not create it.

John Locke (1632-1704)

Locke's most famous work was his *Second Treatise of Civil Government*. It was primarily in this work that Locke advanced his theory of natural law.

For Locke, man was naturally born free, he had a natural liberty where he was equal with all other men, and naturally independent.[76] Locke's recognition of the principle of equality was grounded in reality—he recognized that there are differences in each individual person as to abilities and qualities, but that such differences did not defeat the basic equality of each person.[77] In this state of nature, all men had the perfect freedom to do as they saw fit—in this sense, all men were equal.[78] However, this state of liberty did not amount to a license to do anything.[79] This state of liberty was a state of being

[74] M.M. Goldsmith, "Hobbes on Law" in *The Cambridge Companion to Hobbes* 285-87 (Tom Sorell, ed., Cambridge 1996).

[75] Carl Joachim Friedrich, *The Philosophy of Law in Historical Perspective* 91 (Chicago 1963).

[76] John Locke, *First Treatise of Civil Government*, 4-5; John Locke, *Second Treatise of Civil Government*, 21, 95.

[77] *Second Treatise of Civil Government*, 54.

[78] *Second Treatise of Civil Government*, 4.

[79] *Second Treatise of Civil Government*, 6.

such that each person had the right to be free from oppression and tyranny.[80]

The law of nature, for Locke, was a law of reason. Even though all men were equal and independent, the law of nature required that no one ought to harm another in their life, health, liberty, or property. Further, the law of nature mandated that each person was required to preserve the life, health, liberty, and property of other persons.[81] There were, however, exceptions to this principle of do no harm.

First, each person had the right to punish another for transgressing the natural law.[82] The purpose of any such punishment was limited to: 1) punishment to restrain the offender and prevent repetition of the offense and 2) reparation to the victim for harm done. Essentially, the law of nature allowed for the shedding of a man's blood if that man shed the blood of another.[83] Second, each person had the right to self-defense[84] and to the defense of humanity.[85] This right of self-defense extended to the right to revolt against a tyrannical leader.[86]

In its practical application, the natural law was dependent upon the society and community of man and established governments. The reason for this dependence was the fallibility of human beings and the likelihood of corruption.[87] Despite this dependence on the community, Locke was still recognized as an individualist and it was the individual that was of the greatest importance under the natural law.[88]

Locke recognized that nature was dangerous.[89] Men naturally entered society to ensure peace, safety, and the public good.[90]

[80] *Second Treatise of Civil Government*, 21.
[81] *Second Treatise of Civil Government*, 6
[82] *Second Treatise of Civil Government*, 7.
[83] *Second Treatise of Civil Government*, 8-11.
[84] *Second Treatise of Civil Government*, 233.
[85] *Second Treatise of Civil Government*, 127-30.
[86] *Second Treatise of Civil Government*, 233.
[87] *Second Treatise of Civil Government*, 13.
[88] Heinrich A. Rommen, *The Natural Law, A Study in Legal and Social History and Philosophy* 78-79 (Liberty Fund 1998).
[89] *Second Treatise of Civil Government*, 123.
[90] *Second Treatise of Civil Government*, 131.

The three specific reasons that Locke recognized for men to unite in a community and form a government were: 1) the protection of property,[91] 2) to obtain an unbiased judge when violations of the natural law were alleged,[92] and 3) to support, by the force of the community, the expectation of justice.[93] Locke was a realist in that he recognized that, even in the state of nature, some men were stronger than others and the force of the community might be necessary to equitably enforce the natural law. Thus, the power that men possessed in a state of nature that they ceded to the community was recognized as political power.[94]

Locke recognized that for a man to enter a society or community, he had to surrender his powers under the natural law.[95] By becoming a member of a community, each man consented to the will of the majority of the community.[96] Although, ideally, each man should individually assent to becoming a member of a community, in those instances where a person enjoyed or possessed property under the protection of a community, that person tacitly accepted the rules of that community.[97]

Although Locke recognized that governments were necessary to ensure the equal and universal application of the natural law, he also recognized that human beings who occupied positions of authority in government were quite fallible. The ultimate goal of any government, under the natural law, was the good of the people.[98] Accordingly, Locke suggested four limitations (i.e., subordinate natural laws) on governments.

The first limitation was that the government was limited to legislating laws to preserve society in accordance with the public good.[99] Essentially, under the natural law, the ceding of power to the

[91] *Second Treatise of Civil Government*, 124.
[92] *Second Treatise of Civil Government*, 125.
[93] *Second Treatise of Civil Government*, 126.
[94] *Second Treatise of Civil Government*, 171.
[95] *Second Treatise of Civil Government*, 88-91.
[96] *Second Treatise of Civil Government*, 96-99.
[97] *Second Treatise of Civil Government*, 119.
[98] *Second Treatise of Civil Government*, 229.
[99] *Second Treatise of Civil Government*, 134.

community by its constituent members did not give the government the right to destroy property, enslave the populace, or impoverish the people.[100]

The second limitation was that a law could not be arbitrary or unjust.[101] By this limitation, Locke meant that the government must dispense justice under standing laws. Further, these laws had to be universal and applicable to all people, to reflect the equality of the state of nature.[102] The standard of measuring the validity of human laws was that they had to be evaluated against the natural law and God's laws. Even rulers were subject to the natural law.[103] The exercise of absolute or arbitrary power without the corresponding natural right was a tyranny and a violation of the natural law.[104] The use of force was justified in the removal of such a tyranny.[105] Commentators have recognized that Locke's theory of justified revolt was not just a theoretical exercise but a practical application of the natural law.[106]

The third limitation was that any government could not exist without the consent of the people governed.[107] If the legislative entity, even if it was elected, permitted an executive to exercise tyrannical power, the legislative entity forfeited its power and all power devolved to the people to resume their natural state of liberty.[108] The fourth limitation was that the legislative function could not be delegated to another entity or body.[109] Despite these apparently practical limits on the problem of applying natural law, they have not been recognized as workable.[110]

[100] *Second Treatise of Civil Government,* 135.
[101] *Second Treatise of Civil Government,* 136-37.
[102] *Second Treatise of Civil Government*, 21.
[103] *Second Treatise of Civil Government*, 195.
[104] *Second Treatise of Civil Government*, 172.
[105] *Second Treatise of Civil Government*, 199, 204.
[106] Richard Ashcroft, "Locke's Political Philosophy" in *The Cambridge Companion to Locke* 226-51 (Vere Chappell, ed., Cambridge 1994).
[107] *Second Treatise of Civil Government,* 138.
[108] *Second Treatise of Civil Government*, 222.
[109] *Second Treatise of Civil Government*, 141.
[110] Carl Joachim Friedrich, *The Philosophy of Law in Historical Perspective* 104 (Chicago 1963).

Throughout his work, Locke made numerous references to the work of God and divine law. However, these references did not change the ultimate basis of the natural law which, for Locke, was reason. Accordingly, Locke's theory of natural law falls within that category of natural law that is dependent on reason.

Baron Charles De Montesquieu (1689-1755)

Montesquieu is best known for his work *The Spirit of Laws*. Montesquieu recognized that men are governed by a number of different laws: the law of nature, the divine law, the canon law, the law of nations, the political law both general and particular, the law of conquest, the civil law, and the domestic law.[111] Montesquieu also recognized the forms of such laws, such as the positive or written law.[112]

The divine law was the law of God and the canon law the statutory law of the church. The law of nations was the civil law between nations themselves, whereas the civil law was the law that regulated the rights of citizens to defend themselves and their property within their own nation. The domestic law concerned the law of families. The general political law encompassed the principles under which societies were formed and the particular political law concerned each specific society.[113]

The law of nature encompassed those principles which were not reduced to written laws but which applied to man in his natural state. It was the law that existed entirely independent from the framework and existence of human beings.[114] Montesquieu provided a number of examples for the application of the law of nature. The law of nature, according to Montesquieu, permitted a man to defend himself. In a criminal prosecution, the right to confront witnesses against oneself was derivative of the right to self-defense and, thus, the law of nature, as was the right to present evidence in one's own

[111] Montesquieu, *The Spirit of Laws*, Book XXVI, 1.
[112] *The Spirit of Laws*, Book I, 3.
[113] *The Spirit of Laws*, Book XXVI, 1.
[114] *The Spirit of Laws*, Book I, 2.

behalf. Also within the scope of the natural law was the right to marry and divorce—a third party did not have the right to force a marital separation. Further, it was against the law of nature for one family member to testify against another in a criminal prosecution. Under the natural law, children were obligated to support fathers who had fallen into poverty. And, fathers were required to provide for their children, even though it did not require them to make them heirs. Reflecting the modern notion of sexual equality, Montesquieu considered it a violation of the natural law for daughters to be denied the right to inherit, where sons were allowed to do so. Interestingly, Montesquieu felt that the law of nature of self-defense was superior to the precepts of religion, where the religious requirements resulted in a weakening of the nation.[115]

Essentially, Montesquieu acknowledged four laws of nature: peace based on fear, nourishment, sex, and society with other men based on man's natural ability to acquire knowledge.[116] The ever important right to self-defense was dependent upon the law of nature of peace. It was under the law of nature that men were naturally independent.[117] In nature, all men were equal[118] and had unfettered liberty. Indeed, the principle of equality was a fundamental value for Montesquieu and his understanding of individual liberty.[119]

Most instructive for the concept of liberty under the law of nature, was Montesquieu's view that a state of nature implied that the use of force for political ends was proper.[120] What separated the free and civilized man from the brutal circumstance of nature was the presence of laws, which regulate the society. When men formed a society, natural equality was lost, but the law restored it.[121] However, this was not the end of Montesquieu's exposition on the idea of natural law.[122]

[115] *The Spirit of Laws*, Book XXVI, 3-7.
[116] *The Spirit of Laws*, Book I, 2.
[117] *The Spirit of Laws*, Book XXVI, 15.
[118] *The Spirit of Laws*, Book VIII, 3.
[119] *The Spirit of Laws*, Book V, 3-5.
[120] *The Spirit of Laws*, Book XXVI, 20.
[121] *The Spirit of Laws*, Book VIII, 3.
[122] *The Spirit of Laws*, Book XXVI, 20.

The political law referred to the establishment of a society and the object of that society. The ultimate object of a society is the safety of its people.[123] Further, it was based on the idea of justice for all the people.[124] It was under the political law that men obtained liberty[125] and, thus, regained their natural equality that was lost on the formation of a society.[126] The political law was based on human reason,[127] although Montesquieu has been considered to be more nature-oriented than reason-oriented in reference to natural law.[128] The exercise of free will, through reason, on application of the political law, was what re-established and maintained liberty for each individual.[129] In contrast, it was the civil law that concerned property. Essential to the political law was the principle that the good of the individual should never give way to the good of the public, except where it concerned individual liberty.[130] Individual liberty was paramount. Under the political law, the people had the right to change the government when the government became destructive of the body politic.[131] Montesquieu's political law encompassed points that other philosophers considered part of the natural law.

Thus, under Montesquieu's philosophy, natural law recognized such basic rights or qualities as peace through reason, nourishment, sex, and society. Montesquieu's right to self-defense extended to the right to preserve individual liberties and remove a government which became destructive of society's goals, which was protection of individual liberty. However, the good life under Montesquieu's theory of natural law was, like Aristotle's theory, based upon a life of moderation.[132]

[123] *The Spirit of Laws*, Book XXVI, 23.
[124] Carl Joachim Friedrich, *The Philosophy of Law in Historical Perspective* 105 (Chicago 1963).
[125] *The Spirit of Laws,* Book XXVI, 15.
[126] *The Spirit of Laws*, Book VIII, 3.
[127] *The Spirit of Laws*, Book I, 3.
[128] Carl Joachim Friedrich, *The Philosophy of Law in Historical Perspective* 107 (Chicago 1963).
[129] *The Spirit of Laws*, Book XII, 2.
[130] *The Spirit of Laws*, Book XXVI, 15.
[131] *The Spirit of Laws*, Book XXVI, 23.
[132] Carl Joachim Friedrich, *The Philosophy of Law in Historical Perspective* 104-05 (Chicago 1963).

Montesquieu was not just as theoretical philosopher. He tried to find methods to apply the natural law in practical politics. One example of his attempts, which the Founding Fathers adopted, was the separation of the legislative, executive, and judicial functions of government.[133]

Accordingly, Montesquieu falls within the category of natural law that depends upon reason. Although reason was not the determinative factor of what principles of natural law existed, reason was the tool to recognize the natural law and then implement it through the political and civil law.

Sir William Blackstone (1723-1780)

Sir William Blackstone was one of the most renowned legal scholars of Great Britain. During the 1700s, he was a professor of law at Oxford University, where he published his famous *Commentaries on the Laws of England*, which presented his theory of natural law. Blackstone was probably the most widely read legal scholar in the colonies prior to and during the American Revolution.[134]

Blackstone's statement of the natural law, which was the will of the maker of the universe, rested on the principle that man had free-will and that any exercise of that free-will should be subject to the natural law.[135] The natural law was superior to any man-made law and the validity of any man-made law was dependent upon the man-made law's adherence to the natural law.[136] Human laws were necessary to enforce the natural law because reason was frequently clouded or corrupt.[137]

Under the natural law, each man had the right to act as he saw fit, bound only by the natural law. Under the natural law, each person had absolute rights and relative rights that were based in

[133] Max Farrand, *The Framing of the Constitution of the United States* 49 (Yale 1913).

[134] Albert Alschuler, *Rediscovering Blackstone*, 145 U. Pa. L. Rev. 1, 4-5 (1996).

[135] Sir William Blackstone, *I Commentaries on the Laws of England* 39-40 (Legal Classics 1983).

[136] *I Commentaries on the Laws of England* 41.

[137] *I Commentaries on the Laws of England* 43.

both reason and nature. These rights were vested in individual persons by the immutable laws of nature.[138]

Blackstone presented three absolute rights under the natural law. The first was the right to personal security. The right to personal security included the right to: life, health, and reputation. It also included the right to the means to sustain life and health. Further, it included the right to defend against detraction and slander.[139]

The second absolute right was the right to personal liberty. This right permitted each man to reside in the place of his choice. It also prevented a man's imprisonment, except by a lawful judgment of his equals and the law of the land.[140]

The third absolute right was the right to property. This right included the ability to use, enjoy, and dispose of property.[141]

Blackstone, however, was a realist and not just a theoretical philosopher. Although Blackstone acknowledged these three absolute rights under the natural law, he recognized that, given the realities of politics, they could not be enforced without certain other rights. Accordingly, Blackstone presented five auxiliary rights that were required under the natural law to preserve it.

The first auxiliary right included limitations on the legislative power of government.[142] For example, Blackstone recognized that the legislature had to be independent of the executive, else a tyranny would result.[143] Further, the legislators had to be free from corruption and bribery and were expected to exercise independent judgment.[144] Blackstone recognized that elections are frequently subject to improper influence and partiality.[145]

The second auxiliary right was a limitation on the executive power of government.[146] Although Blackstone thought that a

[138] *I Commentaries on the Laws of England* 119-23.

[139] *I Commentaries on the Laws of England* 125-30.

[140] *I Commentaries on the Laws of England* 130-34.

[141] *I Commentaries on the Laws of England* 134-36.

[142] *I Commentaries on the Laws of England* 136.

[143] *I Commentaries on the Laws of England* 149-50.

[144] *I Commentaries on the Laws of England* 172-74.

[145] *I Commentaries on the Laws of England* 186.

[146] *I Commentaries on the Laws of England* 137.

monarchy was the best possible executive form of government to prevent bloodshed in the transition of power, he still recognized that an independent legislative power was a necessary limitation on an unrestrained executive.The third auxiliary right was the right to apply to the courts for the redress of injuries.[147] Each man was allowed to present his complaint to a neutral court for a speedy resolution in accordance with the previously ascertained laws.

The fourth auxiliary right was the right to petition the legislative or executive power for the redress of unusual complaints that could not be addressed by the courts through the current law. The basis for this right was the recognition that human laws could not address all possibilities and that, occasionally extraordinary methods were needed to do justice.[148]

The fifth and final auxiliary was the individual right to keep and bear arms for defense. Blackstone recognized that arms were an essential tool for not only personal self-defense but also for the prevention of oppression and tyranny.[149]

Although Blackstone acknowledged that the natural law was a function of the will of the maker of the universe, he also recognized that reason was necessary for the recognition and application of the natural law. Thus, Blackstone's vision of the natural law fell within that type of the natural law that was primarily dependent upon reason, as opposed to divine mandate.

Summary

Examining these historical presentations of natural law, three major perspectives or approaches are apparently applicable to the topic of this article. One perspective is the theological mandate theory of natural law, as expressed by King James I. As this is a work that examines natural law in the minds of the Founding Fathers and as the Founding Fathers essentially conducted a revolt against the hereditary monarchy of Great Britain, it is apparent that this theory of natural law, at least as expressed by King James I, will

[147] *I Commentaries on the Laws of England* 137-38.

[148] *I Commentaries on the Laws of England* 138-39.

[149] *I Commentaries on the Laws of England* 139-41.

have little presence in the Founding Fathers' minds as a basis for their philosophy and jurisprudence, except as a focus for what was *not* wanted in the establishment of a new nation.

There is a strong argument that the natural law theory of Thomas Aquinas falls within this perspective also.However, the explanation by Aquinas of natural law relies heavily on the use of reason to recognize and apply natural law. Further, Aquinas' idea of natural law explicitly recognizes certain purely natural elements—the sex drive and the instinct to survive—which are not traditionally associated with divine mandates. Thus, Aquinas' theory of natural law falls within both the theological mandate based type and the rational determination based type.

A summation of the theological mandate type of theory of natural law essentially consists of the will of God. As Aquinas' theory of natural law also recognizes rational determination, the elements of his theory will be included in the rational determination type of natural law theory.

The second perspective is that which holds that natural law originates in and is dependent on a non-theistic, non-physical realm. Plato's Theory of Forms is the primary representative theory of natural law for this type. As previously explained, ultimate reality for Plato was the non-physical realm and not the physical universe. However, like Aquinas, Plato recognized the use of reason and rational determination for understanding and applying the natural law.

Harmony with the perfect idea of justice was, for Plato, natural law. Unfortunately, Plato provided little in guidance for what constituted perfect justice or natural law. Thus, where Aquinas presented specifics as to what constituted natural law, Plato did not.

A summation of the non-theistic non-physical theory of natural law essentially consists of harmony with the realm of forms. As Plato did not provide specific statements of principles for the natural law, it is almost impossible to practically evaluate this type of natural law theory to the topic of this thesis. The documents written by the Founding Fathers—the Declaration of Independence, the Constitution, and the Bill of Rights—make no reference to the Platonic forms and no reference, direct or implied, is found in the writings of the Founding Fathers, such as *The Federalist Papers*.

The third perspective on natural law is that type which depends upon reason and rational determination. The first proponent of natural law of this type was Aristotle. Aristotle recognized that the natural law had to be universally applied to all people and that it was based on reason. Cicero, like Aristotle, recognized that the natural law was universal and should be applied to all. For Cicero, those traditional laws, such as those which prohibit such acts as murder and theft, would be transgressions of the natural law.

Aquinas, despite his reliance on theological principles, acknowledged that the natural law stood alone. Aquinas presented the following principles as natural law: 1) do good and avoid evil, 2) right to self-preservation, 3) natural instincts such as sex, and 4) use of reason is good and should be used to attain knowledge. Grotius' theory of natural law depended upon rational determination and presented the following principles of natural law: 1) power over one self, 2) right to own property, 3) right of self-defense, 4) obligation not to harm others, and 5) to demand what was due and render what was due. Grotius' theory of natural law depended upon doing what was moral. Hobbes' theory of natural law also depended upon reason. The essential principle of Hobbes' theory of natural law was self-preservation, which was not based on any higher good but on reason and self-interest. Hobbes presented several subordinate laws of nature to ensure self-preservation of all people of which four are essential: 1) work for peace whenever possible, 2) surrender of a portion of one's right liberty and all property, 3) keep one's promise, and 4) employ equity in dealing with other people. Locke, Montesquieu, and Blackstone, as relatively close contemporaries of the Founding Fathers, were probably the most important influences on the Founding Fathers. Locke relied on reason. The principles of natural law propounded by Locke were: 1) preservation of one's own life, health, liberty, and property, 2) preservation of the life, health, liberty, and property of others, 3) right to self-defense against others and oppressive tyranny, and 4) right to punish others for the violation of the natural law. Locke noted that there were subordinate natural laws that applied when men entered into a community and formed a government. These were: 1) laws could only be legislated to protect the public good and could not be used to destroy property, enslave the populace, or impoverish the people, 2) laws could not be unjust or arbitrary and rulings had to be under standing laws, 3) any government could not exist without the consent of the governed, and 4) the legislative authority could not be delegated.

For Montesquieu, who based his theory of natural law on reason, all men were equal and independent under the natural law. Montesquieu presented four natural laws applicable to men: 1) peace based on fear, which included the right of self-defense and the right to remove a tyranny, 2) nourishment, 3) sex, and 4) society with other men. Under the natural law, when men enacted positive laws, these positive laws could not infringe upon a person's individual liberty.

Blackstone, a contemporary of the Founding Fathers, was likely the most influential of all of the modern philosophers. Although Blackstone, like the other modern philosophers, recognized God, he also relied on reason and rational determination for the recognition and application of the natural law. Blackstone presented three absolute rights under the natural law: 1) personal security, 2) personal liberty, and 3) personal property. To effectuate these rights, Blackstone recognized five auxiliary rights: 1) limits on the legislative function, 2) limits on the executive function, 3) right to apply to independent courts for redress of injuries under standing laws, 4) right to apply to the executive or legislative entities for justice where the law and courts were not able to provide justice, and 5) the right to keep and bear arms to defend oneself.

In summation, under the reason and rational determination type of natural law (recognizing the influences of the other types of natural law), the following general principles of natural law can be gleaned from the major philosophers who likely influenced the Founding Fathers.

1. The right to fulfill one's natural physical inclinations, such as sex and food (Aquinas, Grotius, Hobbes, Montesquieu).

2. The right to self-preservation and self-defense, which includes the right to resist tyranny (Aquinas, Grotius, Hobbes, Locke, Montesquieu, Blackstone).

3. The ultimate importance of individual liberty and the right of power over one-self and to self-determination (Grotius, Hobbes, Locke, Montesquieu, Blackstone).

4. The essential equality of all humans (Hobbes, Locke, Montesquieu, Blackstone).

5. The right to personal property and peace and order in society (Hobbes, Locke, Montesquieu, Blackstone).

6. The ultimate good of the use of reason (Aquinas, Grotius, Locke, Montesquieu).

7. The duty to do good and enforce justice (Aquinas, Grotius, Locke, Montesquieu).

8. The universality of the natural law, in that it applies to all humans and the government (Aquinas, Grotius, Hobbes, Locke, Montesquieu).

9. Practical limitations on government, to include: the separation of legislative, executive, and judicial functions; enactment of laws in accord with the natural law and justice; the right to just adjudication of violations of previously established law; the right to petition for the redress of grievances; and the principle that governments should not exist without the consent of the governed—all in protection of individual liberty and the advancement of justice and the common good (Aquinas, Locke, Montesquieu, Blackstone).

These nine essential principles of natural law represent the core of natural law theory of the major philosophers who most likely influenced the Founding Fathers. Although I did not list each and every philosopher I addressed in the first part of my thesis after each general principle of natural law, it is, no doubt correctly, presumed that the philosophers I did list relied upon the works of the previous philosophers.

DISCUSSION

As with any philosophical issue, there are supporters and there are detractors. Natural law is no different. The existence of natural law is anathema to many conservative legal and philosophical scholars, conservative politicians, and conservative jurists. Conservatives decry the use of natural law as a figment of a deficient intellect with no foundation in fact or law.

Thus, the question is: Does the natural law exist in American legal and political philosophy and jurisprudence? A number of scholars consider the answer to this question self-evident.[150] Moreover, there are a number of references to the natural law in the writings of the Founding Fathers even before the enactment of the Constitution and the Bill of Rights.[151] As this is America and as the philosophy and application of legal principles in America is supposed to be based on the Declaration of Independence, the Constitution, and the Bill of Rights, an examination of these documents for the existence of natural law seems appropriate.

There are numerous references to the background of the Founding Fathers, as to their education and the philosophers that they read. Generally, the Founding Fathers read the ancient Greek and Roman classics. They read Locke, Montesquieu, and Blackstone.[152] Locke was a primary influence on all the Founding Fathers.[153] Grotius' and Locke's individualistic natural law philosophy was recognized as a profound influence on the American colonies in their formative years.[154] Montesquieu's work was, according to one famous scholar, considered to be the political gospel of the Founding Fathers.[155] Regardless of these other jurisprudential giants, Blackstone was considered the ultimate authority on law at that time. For example, he was extensively quoted by Richard Henry Lee and Samuel Adams.[156] Blackstone was, simply stated, the ultimate legal authority for the Founding Fathers. He significantly influenced the Declaration of Independence, the Constitution, and the Bill of Rights.[157]

[150] Christopher Collier & James Lincoln Collier, *Decision in Philadelphia: The Constitutional Convention of 1787*, 332-50 (Ballantine 1986).

[151] Thomas Paine, *Common Sense*, 38 (Signet Classics 2003). Thomas Paine, *The Rights of Man*, 166-70 (Signet Classics 2003). Thomas Paine, *The Rights of Man*, 217-21 (Signet Classics 2003) (quoting the *Declaration of the Rights of Man and Citizens by the Nationa Assembly of France*).

[152] Forrest McDonald, *The Formation of the American Republic 1776-1790* 72, 157 (Penquin 1965).

[153] Leonard W. Levy, *Origins of the Bill of Rights* 251-52 (Yale 1999).

[154] J.B. Schneewind, "Locke's Moral Philosophy" in *The Cambridge Companion to Locke* 222 (Vere Chappell, ed., Cambridge 1994).

[155] Max Farrand, *The Framing of the Constitution of the United States* 49 (Yale 1913).

[156] David Hutchinson, *The Foundations of the Constitution* 320-21 (University Books 1975).

[157] Albert Alschuler, *Rediscovering Blackstone*, 145 U. Pa. L. Rev. 1, 15-16 (1996).

Numerous works recognize the influence of fundamental, or natural, law on the Founding Fathers when they were drafting the Constitution,[158] although the church and the English common law were also recognized as strong influences. It must be remembered that the primary chronicler of the English common law, however, was Blackstone who, as previously explained, was a natural law adherent. Thus, any differences between the English common law and the natural law are blurred in any analysis of the intent of the Founding Fathers. Essentially, natural law cannot be separated from any examination of the intent of the Founding Fathers.[159] Perhaps the best way to determine the existence of natural law and its principles in the minds of the Founding Fathers is to examine the actual political/legal documents that the Founding Fathers wrote. I will apply the foregoing general principles of natural law to the three most important documents penned by the Founding Fathers: the Declaration of Independence, the Constitution, and the Bill of Rights.

The Declaration of Independence

Succinctly stated, the Declaration of Independence was, and still likely is, the ultimate statement of natural law rights in contemporary western civilization. It has been the hope and guiding light of this and other nations.[160] Although most authorities hold the position that the Declaration of Independence is not binding law, in any sense of the term "law," it has been recognized as the quintessentially accurate statement of American political and legal philosophy. As such, it is the ultimate basis for interpretation and application of American law. It cannot be disputed that this document is based on the natural law.

It is interesting to note that many American positivist jurists (i.e., strict constructionists) rely on legislative intent when interpreting law

[158] David Hutchinson, *The Foundations of the Constitution* 7-9, (University Books 1975).
[159] Douglas W. Kmiec, *Natural Law v. Natural Rights: What Are They? How Do They Differ?* 20 *Harv. J.L. & Pub. Pol'y* 627, 649 (1997).
[160] Pauline Maier, *American Scripture: Making the Declaration of Independence* (Knopf 1997).

in their favor, but reject it when this interpretative principle is used to apply and interpret the Constitution by referring to the Declaration of Independence. Although positivism and strict constructionism are not identical, they share many similar characteristics.

The very first sentence of the Declaration of Independence states: "When . . . it becomes necessary for one People to dissolve the Political Bonds which have connected them with another . . . ." This sentence clearly invokes the third principle of natural law of self-determination. It also implicates the second principle of natural law of self-defense from tyranny, although even more evidence of this implication is obtained by the actual political situation of the American colonies, which was a state of revolt.

The first sentence continues with the following phrase: ". . . and to assume among the Powers of the Earth, the separate and equal Station to which the Laws of Nature and of Nature's God entitle them . . . ." This specific reference to natural law is instructive in that it sets the stage for the entire document and the actions of the Founding Fathers. Indeed, this phrase is an essential element of this article, as it clearly and unequivocally specifies the authoritative basis upon which the Founding Fathers acted. But this does not make this article superfluous. In the realm of politics, many claims to such principles as justice and freedom are made, but all too frequently the claims are empty.

The second paragraph of the Declaration of Independence begins with the statement that: "We hold these Truths to be self-evident, that all Men are created equal, that they are endowed by their Creator with certain inalienable Rights, that among these are Life, Liberty, and the Pursuit of Happiness . . . ." The statement that all men are created equal matches the fourth principle of natural law enunciated above. The statement that these rights are inalienable mirrors the eighth principle of natural law, that the natural law is universal and applies to all people. The identification of life as an inalienable (i.e., natural) right restates the first and second principles of natural law stated above. The identification of liberty as an inalienable (i.e., natural) right identically restates the fourth principle of natural law. And, finally, the specification of happiness as an inalienable (i.e., natural) right is clearly equatable with the third principle of natural law of self-determination.

The second paragraph of the Declaration of Independence continues by stating: ". . . That to secure these Rights, Governments are instituted among Men, deriving their just Powers from the Consent of the Governed . . . ." This statement indisputably reflects the ninth principle of natural law previously stated that governments exist for the benefit of men and that they exist only for the benefit of the populace.

This same sentence continues with: ". . . that whenever any Form of Government becomes destructive of these Ends, it is the Right of the People to alter or to abolish it, and to institute new Government, laying its Foundation on such Principles, and organizing its Powers in such Form, as to them shall seem most likely to effect their Safety and Happiness." This phrase acknowledges that the people have the right to revolt against tyranny, which is the second principle of natural law. Further, it acknowledges that the purpose of government is to protect the people, which comports with the ninth principle of natural law, and that it implies that government will have some limits on its powers, which also comports with the ninth principle.

Further, in the same paragraph, the authoring Founding Fathers reiterated their position that a people had the right to revolt against a tyranny, which is a restatement of the second principle of natural law. Indeed, many commentators recognize that the right to revolt, as expressed by Locke, was political orthodoxy at the time of the writing of the Declaration of Independence.[161]

The Founding Fathers then listed their grievances against the King of England. Several of them will be listed below with a corresponding reference to the principle of natural law that was violated by the King's acts. This comparative listing demonstrates the presence of the natural law in the minds of the Founding Fathers when they were attempting to justify the American Revolution.

A. "He has refused his Assent to Laws, the most wholesome and necessary for the public Good"—which is a violation of the ninth principle of natural law that requires the laws to be for the public good.

[161] Pauline Maier, *American Scripture: Making the Declaration of Independence* 134-45 (Knopf 1997).

B. "He has forbidden his Governors to pass Laws of immediate and pressing Importance . . ."—which is a violation of the ninth principle of natural law that implicitly recognizes the need for laws.

C. "He has dissolved Representative Houses repeatedly, for opposing with manly firmness his Invasions on the Rights of the People."—which is a violation of the ninth principle of natural law that requires the separation of the executive and legislative functions.

D. "He has obstructed the Administration of Justice, by refusing his Assent to Laws for establishing the Judiciary Powers."—which is a violation of the ninth principle of natural law that requires the separation of the judicial, executive, and legislative powers and that requires justice to be done.

E. "He has made Judges dependent upon his Will alone . . ."—which is a violation of the ninth principle of natural law that requires the separation of the judicial and executive functions and which requires independent adjudication of grievances.

F. "He has affected to render the Military independent and separate to the Civil Power."—which is a violation of the third principle of natural law that specifies individual liberty to be of ultimate importance and places the tools of tyranny in a superior position to the natural authority of the people.

G. "For quartering large Bodies of Armed Troops among us"—which is a violation of the third principle of natural law that mandates individual liberty and which is a violation of the fifth principle of natural law that allows private property.

H. "For protecting them (the military), by a mock Trial, from Punishment for any Murders which they should commit on the Inhabitants . . . ."—which is a violation of the ninth principle of natural law that requires fair and just adjudications of violations of law.

I. "For cutting of our Trade with all Parts of the World."—which is a violation of the fifth principle of natural law that allows personal property and which is a violation of the third principle of natural law that allows self-determination and individual liberty.

J. "For imposing Taxes on us without our Consent."—which is a violation of the fifth principle of natural law that permits personal property and which is a violation of the ninth principle of natural law that requires just and fair adjudication of grievances and government only with consent.

K. "For suspending our Legislatures, and declaring themselves invested with Power to legislate for us in all Cases whatsoever."—which is a violation of the ninth principle of natural law that requires the separation of the executive and legislative functions and which is a violation of the third principle of natural law that allows self-determination.

This is an essential recognition of all of the principles of natural law recognized by the Founding Fathers, as expressed in, inter alia, the Declaration of Independence, as it is one of the basic methods recognized by the natural law philosophers to ensure the application of the natural law.

L. "He has plundered our Seas, ravaged our Coasts, burnt our Towns, and destroyed the Lives of our People."—which clearly implicates the second principle of natural law that allows self-defense and which is a violation of the fifth principle of natural law that mandates peace and order and personal property.

M. "He has constrained our fellow Citizens taken Captive on the high Seas to bear Arms against their Country . . . ."—which is a violation of the third principle of natural law that mandates the importance of individual liberty.

The Declaration of Independence includes other grievances against the King of England; however, the listed grievances are representative of the violations of natural law that are contained in the document.

Examining these excerpts from the Declaration of Independence, the presence of the principles of natural law in the minds of the Founding Fathers at the time of the writing of the document is undisputable. Indeed, from the overwhelming presence of natural law principles, it can be concluded that there was little else of philosophical import that significantly influenced the Founding Fathers in their endeavors.

The Constitution

Where the Declaration of Independence sets forth the fundamental principles of American political and legal philosophy, the Constitution was the Founding Fathers' attempt to bring these fundamental principles of natural law into practical application. Even though natural law's proper place is, arguably, in the realm of theory and philosophy, evidence of it can be found in the attempts to practically apply it. Indeed, as shown in the previous discussion, Hobbes, Locke, Montesquieu, and Blackstone incorporated practical aspects of the implementation of natural law in their works.

The Preamble of the Constitution states: "We the People of the United States, in Order to form a more perfect Union, establish Justice, insure domestic Tranquility, provide for the common defence, promote the general Welfare, and secure the Blessings of Liberty to ourselves and our Posterity, do ordain and establish this Constitution for the United States of America." The language clearly recognizes the fundamental nature of liberty, which is the third principle of natural law. It also recognizes the principle of justice, which is incorporated in the seventh and ninth principles of natural law. It further recognizes peace and order, which is a right under the fifth principle of natural law. Finally, by its specification that liberty should be preserved for themselves and their posterity, the Founding Fathers recognized the principle of the universality of the document and, thus, the eighth principle of natural law.

The Constitution also recognizes the ninth principle of natural law that a government is valid only if it has the consent of the governed. Article I requires the election of the legislature and Article II requires the election of the executive. These Articles recognize the natural law principle of self-determination.

Further, the actual publications of the Founding Fathers in support of the ratification of the Constitution[162] and the actual personal correspondence of the Founding Fathers are both in accord with the natural law principles expressed in the Declaration of Independence, the Constitution, and the Bill of Rights. Even though some authorities, both natural law and positivist, might argue that

[162] See, e.g., *The Federalist Papers.*

the personal views of the Founding Fathers expressed in their personal correspondence are irrelevant, I reject this position for two reasons: 1) in their correspondence the Founding Fathers specifically discussed the reasons and justification for these documents, and 2) the opinions of the Founding Fathers as to what these documents meant are far superior to any determination of the meaning of these documents by any scholar judging them several centuries later, especially given the complexities, denotations, connotations, nuances, and misinterpretations of language. Thus, I would strongly suggest that any argument that the Founding Fathers' personal views of natural law theory and the Declaration of Independence, the Constitution, and the Bill of Rights are irrelevant is without merit. My position is strongly supported by the contemporary view that the use of legislative intent in the interpretation of statutes is not just acceptable, but almost necessarily must be employed, especially where the written law is vague, unclear, or incomplete. Accordingly, I draw an analogy between the contemporary use of legislative intent and the technique of examining the personal views of the Founding Fathers (i.e., their intent) to determine the meaning of the Declaration of Independence, the Constitution, and the Bill of Rights

The Constitution also specifically rejects the concept of monarchy and the theory of natural law that imposed a divine right of rule, as expressed by King James I. Article I forbids the granting of any title of nobility, which is an implicit recognition of the fourth principle of natural law of the equality of all people.

The Constitution also recognizes the ninth principle of natural law that required the separation of the legislative, executive, and judicial functions. This was accomplished by the creation of three separate respective branches of government.[163] This is an essential recognition of all of the principles of natural law recognized by the Founding Fathers, as expressed in, inter alia, the Declaration of Independence, as it is one of the basic methods recognized by the natural law philosophers to ensure the application of the natural law.

The Founding Fathers recognized that government and the people who occupy government positions are not perfect, which

[163] *United States Constitution*, art. I, II, & III.

was also recognized by many of the natural law philosophers. They made a provision for the removal of corrupt governmental officials by impeachment.[164] This provision is an implicit recognition of the ninth principle of natural law. Indeed, the Constitution and the Bill of Rights express the highest level of corruption in naturalistic terms: the violation of the natural rights of the people.

Thus, although the Constitution is, arguably, a somewhat technical and practical document, its provisions essentially ratified the principles of natural law that were stated in the Declaration of Independence, which has been widely rejected as a legal document. However, even the Founding Fathers recognized the potential for abuse under the Constitution and that the natural rights of the people were not sufficiently protected under it. Accordingly, a Bill of Rights was also enacted.

It is interesting to note that both the liberal and conservative Founding Fathers recognized the existence of rights—they just differed in how they were to be protected. The conservatives (i.e., the Federalists) wanted no Bill of Rights, as it could be interpreted as limiting the natural rights of the people[165] and the liberals (i.e., the Anti-Federalists) wanted a Bill of Rights to protect certain fundamental rights.[166] Some of the Founding Fathers felt that the rights accorded to individuals were created by the written enacted law.[167] However, the vast majority of the Founding Fathers' publications were geared to natural law theory, as evidenced by their heavy reliance on Locke, Montesquieu, and Blackstone, who were indisputably natural law adherents.

Indeed, taking the Constitution as an integrated expression of law and natural rights, and applying both natural law theory and positive law theory to its holistic interpretation, the more accurate

[164] *United States Constitution*, art. I, § 3.

[165] *1 The Founders' Constitution*, ch. 14, Item 29, p. 456 (comments of Robert Whitehall, Pennsylvania Ratifying Convention, 28 Nov. 1787) (Philip B. Kurland & Ralph Lerner, eds., University of Chicago Press 1987).

[166] *1 The Founders' Constitution*, ch. 14, Item 30, p. 456 (letter of Thomas Jefferson to James Madison, 20 Dec. 1787) (Philip B. Kurland & Ralph Lerner, eds., University of Chicago Press 1987).

[167] See *1 The Founders' Constitution*, ch. 14, Item 27, p. 453 (comments of James Wilson at the Pennsylvania Ratifying Convention, 28 Nov. 1787) (Philip B. Kurland & Ralph Lerner, eds., University of Chicago Press 1987).

explanation for its basis is natural law theory. Attempting to interpret and apply the Constitution as a positivistic document simply cannot be effectively accomplished without referring to external principles of morality and justice, which is, essentially, a maxim of natural law. This is shown by the several references to, inter alia, justice and liberty. Neither term is defined in the Constitution nor would either term likely be recognized by a positivist in the context that they are used by the Founding Fathers. The only way to interpret them is to refer to external principles of morality and justice, which would be anathema to a positivist. Thus, the Constitution, as an integrated document, is more compatible with natural law theory.

The Bill of Rights

There has been much discussion as to why there is a Bill of Rights. Under traditional natural law theory, formal legislative recognition of natural rights is not necessary—they exist independently. However, the Founding Fathers were realists. A significant disagreement existed between the Federalists and the Anti-Federalists. The Federalists wanted no written Bill of Rights on the ground that such an enumeration would be construed to limit the people's natural right (which, unfortunately, has apparently occurred today). The Anti-Federalists wanted a written Bill of Rights to ensure that certain fundamental natural rights would not be ignored for the lack of formal recognition.[168] Regardless, both parties recognized the existence of the natural law and the associated rights.[169] A compromise was accomplished by the enactment of the Bill of Rights with the Ninth and Tenth Amendments, which specifically stated that the enumeration of rights did not disparage other rights and that any non-enumerated powers were reserved to the states and the people. Indeed, the Founding Fathers realized that neither the Bill of Rights, nor any other legislative act, could create fundamental natural rights—such a document could only acknowledge them and not create them.[170] I will compare each of

[168] See generally Leonard W. Levy, *Origins of the Bill of Rights* 1-43 (Yale 1999).
[169] Leonard W. Levy, *Origins of the Bill of Rights* 27 (Yale 1999).
[170] Bernard Bailyn, *The Ideological Origins of the American Revolution* 186-89 (Harvard 1992).

the Amendments in the Bill of Rights to the general principles of natural law I previously synthesized.

a. First Amendment

The First Amendment preserves the rights of freedom of speech and the press, freedom of religion, freedom to assemble, and the right to petition the government for the redress of grievances. The right to petition the government is specifically recognized in the ninth principle of natural law. The remaining freedoms all encompass the third principle of natural law of liberty and self-determination. Although they are not specifically stated or mentioned by the philosophers, they can easily be seen to fall into the category of auxiliary rights, necessary for the preservation of the fundamental rights under natural law, as explained by Blackstone. Indeed, the original intent of the Founding Fathers has been recognized to encompass the principle that if a people are to be self-governing, in accordance with the ninth principle of natural law, they need accurate information upon which to base their votes, and this requires the freedom of speech and the press.[171]

b. Second Amendment

The Second Amendment is an express reservation of the right under the natural law to revolt when a tyrannical government occurs. Although many modern authorities argue otherwise, the history of the American Revolution and the Second Amendment indisputably shows that this was the intent of the Founding Fathers when they enacted it.[172] If nothing else, the Second Amendment is a very practical solution to the problem of a tyranny. The right to revolt is a specific right under natural law theory that the Declaration of Independence and the Second Amendment recognize.

[171] Stanley C. Brubaker, "Original Intent and Freedom of Speech and Press" in *The Bill of Rights, Original Meaning and Current Understanding* 89 (Eugene W. Hickok, Jr., ed., Virginia 1991).

[172] Wm. C. Plouffe, Jr., "A Federal Court Holds the Second Amendment is an Individual Right: Jeffersonian Utopia or Apocalypse Now?" 30 *U. Mem. L. Rev.* 55 (1999).

c. Third Amendment

The Third Amendment provides protection against the unwilling quartering of troops in civilian homes. Essentially, this amendment is a protection of private property, which is the fifth principle of natural law. It also implicitly protects liberty under the third principle of natural law.

d. Fourth Amendment

The Fourth Amendment protects the individual people against unreasonable searches and seizures of their persons and in their homes and property. Essentially, the Fourth Amendment is the quintessential practical protection of liberty and property, as recognized by the third and fifth principles of natural law. As a practical matter, the Founding Fathers were concerned about the actual application of the rights guaranteed by the Fourth Amendment. By the very words of the Fourth Amendment, they expressed a preference for a warrant when searches and seizures were conducted. It was also their position that enforcement would be accomplished through the common law which, as shown by the discussion of Blackstone, who was the primary chronicler of the English common law, was an expression of natural law.[173] The Tenth Amendment specifically reserves any power not specifically enumerated in the Bill of Rights to the state or the people. This is an express recognition, in accord with the natural law that all powers, and rights, originally lie with the people.

e. Fifth Amendment

The Fifth Amendment provides several protections to ensure a fair trial that include: protection from double jeopardy, protection from being a witness against oneself in a criminal trial, and protection from being charged with a serious crime except upon indictment by a grand jury. A fair trial is mandated under the ninth principle of

[173] Bradford P. Wilson, "The Fourth Amendment as More Than a Form of Words: The View From the Founding" in *The Bill of Rights, Original Meaning and Current Understanding* 151-71 (Eugene W. Hickok, Jr., ed., Virginia 1991).

natural law. Further, the seventh principle of natural law mandates that justice be done, which this amendment's protections attempt to facilitate. The Fifth Amendment also specifically protects life, liberty, and property and prohibits their taking without due process of law. This phrase encompasses the first, second, third, and fifth principles of natural law. The Fifth Amendment and the Fourth Amendment are complementary in that the Fifth Amendment specifically expresses and protects the essential principles of natural rights and the Fourth Amendment provides practical application of the natural rights. Scholars have recognized that the intent of the Founding Fathers as to due process of law encompassed the procedural rights due to a person under the common law before a conviction or punishment would be had.[174] And, as it was Blackstone who was the authoritative source of the common law, as an expression of the natural law, it is evident that the natural law was the source of these protections.

f. Sixth Amendment

The Sixth Amendment guarantees the right to a speedy, public, and impartial trial by a jury of one's peers in a criminal prosecution and the right to be confronted with opposing witnesses, the right to compulsory process to obtain witnesses, and the right to counsel. These rights are encompassed within the ninth principle of natural law and are practical subsidiary rights which allow the protection and enforcement of the other principles of natural law. This Amendment also encompasses the seventh principle of natural law which is to do justice.

g. Seventh Amendment

The Seventh Amendment preserves the right to a jury trial. This right is within the ninth principle of natural law that mandates a fair trial.

[174] Christopher Wolfe, "The Original Meaning of the Due Process Clause" in *The Bill of Rights, Original Meaning and Current Understanding* 213-30 (Eugene W. Hickok, Jr., ed., Virginia 1991).

h. Eighth Amendment

The Eighth Amendment prohibits cruel and unusual punishments, excessive fines, and excessive bail. Essentially, this Amendment recognizes the natural law rights to liberty, property, and justice under the third, fifth, and seventh principles of natural law.

i. Ninth and Tenth Amendments

The Ninth Amendment implicitly recognizes that the people have other rights in addition to those specifically enumerated. Although this Amendment does not specifically state any particular right or protection, it can be soundly argued that it is an explicit recognition of the existence of additional rights retained by the people under the natural law.[175] The Tenth Amendment specifically reserves any power not specifically enumerated in the Bill of Rights to the state or the people. This is an express recognition, in accord with the natural law that all powers, and rights, originally lie with the people.[176]

These Amendments are the most powerful implicit recognition and expression of natural law in the Bill of Rights. They specifically acknowledge the existence of other rights, in addition to those not specifically enumerated, which is an essential element of natural law theory. Indeed, some of the Founding Fathers (i.e., James Madison and Alexander Hamilton) even specifically referred to them under the theory of natural law when arguing for the adoption of the Constitution and the Bill of Rights.[177] Moreover, there are many specific references in common law scholarship and jurisprudence to the natural law.[178]

[175] *The Rights Retained by the People: The History and Meaning of the Ninth Amendment* (Randy E. Barnett, ed., George Mason University Press 1989).

[176] Eugene W. Hickok, Jr., "The Original Understanding of the Tenth Amendment" in *The Bill of Rights, Original Meaning and Current Understanding* 455 (Eugene W. Hickok, Jr., ed., Virginia 1991).

[177] David Hutchinson, *The Foundations of the Constitution*, 317 (Univ. Books 1975).

[178] See, e.g., William Blackstone, *Commentaries on the Laws of England* and *Calder v. Bull*, 3 U.S. (3 Dall.) 386 (1795) (Chase, J.).

Overall Interpretation

Some of the Founding Fathers were of the opinion that, as a general matter, rights were created by the sovereign (i.e., the people). This position can be argued for the first eight Amendments in the Bill of Rights, at least individually. However, the majority of the Founding Fathers did not hold to this view.

Examining the Bill of Rights in an holistic manner, and interpreting and applying it as an integrated document, it is an acknowledgment of the basic inherent rights of all people and recognizes the existence of additional unenumerated rights, which is basic natural law theory. Such an interpretation would be directly contradictory to positive law theory.

CONCLUSION

This article is not an exposition to argue the actual existence of the natural law. Rather, it presumed the existence of the natural law. For the purposes of this article, it is irrelevant if the natural law exists as a separate ontological entity or merely as a moral construct based upon the reason and universal morality of human beings.

The problem that is presented was the existence of the natural law in American legal and political philosophy. The Founding Fathers did not write the Declaration of Independence, the Constitution, and the Bill of Rights documents in a vacuum. Given the demonstration of similarities between the principles in these documents and the principles of natural law at the time of the writing of these documents, it is apparent that natural law was the primary influence on the Founding Fathers and the establishment of the United States of America. Not only did natural law influence American legal and political philosophy, it was actually directly incorporated into American legal and political philosophy.

Virginia Black

THE RIGHTNESS OF REASON

Right reason (*recta ratio*) is universal and enduring. Its forms are numerous. The orderliness in nature that it seeks is pervasive. No wonder the Greeks called man the rational creature: just consider the delineation of the powers and projects of reason! Consider the many ways in which right reason puts order into reality and discovers the orders that are already there. Consider, too, the rigorous use of its many practical implications. Right reason intuits essences (*eidos*), both natural and created by human choice. Alert to proportion and pattern, right reason describes the kosmos, or general order, of these essences. Right reason performs induction; it gathers up (*synagoge)* repetitions and resemblances (*homoios*) from nature's parts, identifying them as universals—as series species, sequences, sets weighing their similarities, excluding their differences. When through right reason these universals are brought into lawful relation (*analogia*) to each other, unity and a larger coherence occur. The laws of nature (*phusis*) reflect the truth (*aletheia*) about this larger coherence. The practical reason discerns (*aisthesis*) the most adaptive paths to help us determine the most intelligent ends (*sophrosyne*) to pursue.

Consider also right reason's power to organize abstractions (*logistikon*). To do this, right reason must understand itself; it must self-consciously screen out (*aphairesis*) the substance of objects, leaving only the forms and their relations. Thus it accomplishes a priori analysis, demonstration (*scientia*) of that which is immediately apprehended (*nous*), logic (*logos*), and deduction from first principles (*episteme*). Hence right reason, both through theory (*theoria*) and practice, imparts consistency and wholeness (*holon*) to our knowledge of nature's things and orders.

Ethics and law limit and define this knowledge of nature's things and orders, preparing it for human adoption. Along with nature's laws, we now may speak of nature's rules (*nomoi*). Right reason applied to morals and to positive laws (*sophia*) exhibits the same outcome as when applied to nature's physical laws. It exhibits principled order. Principled order would not be possible if justice were not the ground of law. The same good reasons that make order lawful also make order moral. Impartiality of judgment, acting on right principle, objectivity in appraising facts, seeking rational coherence between ideas, these are the organizing principles of both morality and nature, of both value and law.

Consider now, again, the many ways in which right reason discovers the details of this practical knowledge (*prudentia*), how more precisely it regulates the governance of human conduct through nature's rules. (1) Justice itself means equality of treatment, impartiality of judgment–no preference, no privilege, no prejudice to confuse the orderliness of the rule. (2) The rule of law brings everyone alike under its norm: same offense, same treatment. (3) Just punishment must stand in right relation, it must stand in balance with its corresponding wrong. (4) Just desserts are even-handed: correction, compensation, equity (*epieikela*)—these bring right reasoning to matters that have lost proportion. (5) Rules of reason called precedents measure similarity and repetition in persons' circumstances, resemblances and likenesses that assure adjudication procedures are evenly balanced. (6) Universalizability assures that these cases are not arbitrarily disposed, egotistically evaluated, irrationally resolved. (7) "The reasonable man" provides law with a standard of practical judgment (*phronesis*) in order to assess what is expectable and so, what in ordinary circumstances is prudent and fair. (8) Practical reasoning in law (*noesis*) requires that the components used to arrive at judgment be relevant to the case.

These insights into the theoretical and applied workings of right reason may lead us to a reality we previously ignored. Right reason may one day discover a legal ethic, conferring upon us a just and rational system (*systema*) to which all persons can beneficially repair. If physical and social reality were different, right reason could not participate in knowledge. If resemblance and regularity, balance and proportion, ratio and rule (*symmetria*) were not the elements of enduring order in nature, right reason could not aspire to understand the harmonious orders of science, of action, morality and law. It could not comprehend the whole of things. All would exclude it—the applied and the transcendent, the common and the path breaking.

There is no avoiding *recta ratio*. In dialect with itself and the world, *recta ratio* puts us in touch with the conception of an ordered reality *sub specie aeternitatis*. It both formulates and composes the laws of nature and the natural law.

Vera Lex, Vol. III, No. 2, 1982

HOW VARIABLE IS NATURAL LAW?

At least since Vico, it has been usual for moderns to declare that natural law is a dynamic and developing idea. Aquinas acknowledged that the "determinations" of natural law, like individuals within a species, are varied and distinctive; and even fundamental norms can be modified in light of cultural change and circumstance. Montesquieu appreciated the manifold of conditions that shape the interpretation and affectability of morals and law. Burke was insistent that the social conditions of the times modify institutional forms even of fundamental principles; not theory but historical experience stands as the basis of the ethical. Vico spoke of natural law with a changing content.

Why these defensive concessions? Why is it not crystal clear that First Principles in morals not only prohibit egregious wrongs but are also used as guides in problematic moral reasoning and proposals? This necessarily makes their practice resourceful and individuated. It was quite clear to Aristotle. Intellectual virtue, *prudentia*, already suggested that in the unfolding of moral activity and in the development toward actualization, we should look to the particulars of time and place and person. The Roman "law of the peoples" even in its search for the commonalities of group life yet respected the differentials that define a culture. Why, then, has it been thought necessary to defend variation and accident along with substance and essence when these complementing pairs had often been enunciated and attempts had been made to explain their mutually assisting function? What happened in between to make it necessary to emphasize the developmental character of natural law? Possibly natural law as an eternal, immutable principle found sympathy in the Stoics' Ordering Principle that "governs the whole," in their unchangeable and universally valid Natural Law of Justice, or in their belief in a human inclination toward the proper act and end. The orientation toward certainty and permanence as a test of knowledge was of course strongly prefigured in Plato. Perhaps the concept grew in this direction under Christian thought as it congealed in doctrine. God is The Good, and from His changeless eternal law springs the ground of natural law. Scotus spoke of a single natural law that one cannot imagine warranted violation or neglect: the commandment to love God. Later on, Cartesianism stressed the rationalistic, deductive conclusions of natural law as possessing, like geometric theorems, the same demonstrative certainty as its First Principles. Here Grotius must be mentioned.

It would seem that, for a time in the history of thought, the One (in contrast to the many), Substance and Essence (in contrast to accident and contingency), the Invisible (in contrast to the visible), the Rational (in contrast to the sensory) got the upper hand. The abstract and the absolute came in. The concrete and the changing went out. But today, and for quite some time now, we are experiencing a revolt against fixity, transcendence, everlastingness, pure reason, in short, against whatever is a-historical, uniform, immutable and non-relative. Have these ideas exhausted their claims and run their course?

Numerous influences, both for better and worse, have driven moderns to an insistence upon the idiosyncratic, the plural and the relative in morals and laws, even though perhaps the locus for them is misplaced and their advantages are exaggerated. First, Science: evidence and experiment, problem and process, provisional uncertainty, trial and error. Second, Reformation: sectarian preference, personalism, toleration. Third, Enlightenment: nature's autonomy, skepticism, materialism, biological and social evolution. Fourth, the rise of nations: plural and independent states, converting along the way the descending powers of unitary and sovereign monarchy to the ascending powers of the disparate democratic mass. Then came the exciting birth of historical studies and the enriching findings of cultural anthropology out of which moral relativism was born.

The Historical School criticized natural law for its abstract voice and neglect of locale, custom, tradition. Utilitarianism criticized natural law for its seeming indifference to the consequences of its rule-bound obligations and its inability to prove its source. The Positive School criticized idealism, the endeavor to legitimate the positive law by an unshapen natural law.

Today the healthier parts of this many-dimensional revolt against fixity seem to be in decline. A moral pathology has set in. Rousseau's notion of the infinite malleability of man, historicist Marxism and socialist utopianism, intellectualism, the materialist theory of history, scientism, moral egoism—these views may represent degenerate forms of the quite timely and beneficial modifications of dogmatic philosophy and religion insofar as these were linked to rationalism and logic. For if there exists an inflexible system of rationally deducible moral law, then anyone can claim to know and manipulate it. Thus in the 17th century King James I of England declared, "Methinks I hath as much reason as any other man" in justification of his absolute power. Was it not time for a breath of fresh air—time to examine the visible and the sensory, the many and the particular, the process and the variation? Was it not time to give equal time to nature and her flux, to history and her social experiments, to the genetic development of human institutions? What is incidental is often pregnant with implication. The insights of the Hebrew prophets carried a sweeping universal meaning only because their voices were aimed at singular historical moments, making their messages relevant and heard. They embodied ethical ideals in their unique personhood. Let us not be alarmed. Behind the process, science still looks for pattern and law. In variation, evolution still looks for what is potential and continuous; species and kinds have not gone out of favor. However fractured, sectarianism still looks for the spirit behind the flesh. Nevertheless, art and image, symbol and metaphor, the visual models have glided into modern history and remain there with correct and remarkable rectitude. There is danger in absolutizing too abstract an idea. It is the danger that *any* particular can be justified as determined by it—the peril of relativism—for there is no way to show that a determination is false. Paradoxically, it is also the danger that no particular can be justified as determined by it—the peril of ignorance and ambivalence.

It is important, therefore, to retain a close idea of moral substance while watching its institutional history and what the facts are. Admittedly the idea carries a high degree of abstractness; yet it does outline the fact that there exist determinate rights, duties and normative practices with justifiable content. We need only contrast moral substance with Kantian morality in its extreme aspect of formal rationality. "These fundamental principles of morality must originate entirely a priori . . . . they can expect nothing from the inclination of men . . . . In morals . . . the principle of action [is free] from all influences from contingent grounds which only experience can fashion" (*Metaphysics of Morals*). Gone fully is "nature" suggesting specific content to moral laws. Gone is the virtue of prudence as reasonableness that keeps the complex gradations of practical moral judgment in touch with what actually exists.

There is wisdom in the idea that morals and law are dynamic institutions, proof of their origin in nature so long as this healthy friendship with the empirical does not imply that in application anything goes. Hence there is wisdom also in not giving in to the indeterminate and the shifting. Morals and law cannot be anything that anyone declares; and this, I think, was always behind the "unchanging and universal" language of the natural law: It is meant to affirm that no human authority can change at will what is an outgrowth of the experience of man.

Vera Lex, Vol. V, No. 1, 1985

PRINCIPLES AND PRACTICES

...among visible things equivalents for the vision within.
—Rilke, *The Notebook of Malta Laurids Brigge*

On a memorable day this past February, Anatoly Sharansky, exemplifying an historic moment, walked across Berlin's Glienicke Bridge from captivity to the free West. He had been held prisoner in the Soviet Union for engaging in nonviolent dissent. Under a negotiated release, he is now in Israel, the country of his choice. Freedom of migration—and of trade, speech and conscience—is not an untried idea derived from abstract principle and empty slogan. Like any other fundamental moral law, freedom is *in rem*, "in the thing." Its higher order is continuously manifested in existing events, relations, and procedures. As a norm, freedom is invisible so the more important is it that the norm be identified through its corresponding visible activities, roles and organs. Its conceptual or transcendent nature must be acutely realized in a plurality of actual implementations. Sharansky's walk across the bridge illuminated one of these great empirical realizations of freedom.

All sound moral laws complete their meanings in existing situations of one sort or another. They become famed in particulars here and now, in this way or that, so that we come to recognize their diverse forms: voluntary human actions that repeat themselves as anticipations, customs and laws, or that organize themselves as institutes, carrying their ever-growing particularizations through history. If freedom or justice never referred to occurrences either possible or real, they would be worthless ideals. Worse, if through ignorance regarding their growth-ways and structures, they are hastily and forcibly imposed on a people by way of de novo reconstruction, they are exceedingly dangerous. Lacking knowledge of what has worked in the past, it may seem that an ideal for society can mean anything we want to strive for; its urgency seems to demand that we instantly lock it into law. Thus did the Jacobins think "fraternité" meant State terrorism: Kill the bourgeoisie! Then seize and communize their property!

How shall we know to which kinds of activities and orders a theoretical principle can be applied, so that its meaning and necessity are not plundered by incoherence? The clearest procedure for discovering the "proper" instruments belonging to a principle of right is by way of careful observation of social history, taking note of successes and failures in its institutions and their results. Moral ideas have to establish their referents indirectly by a kind of selection and correction until workable networks of peaceable interactions gradually emerge that hold a bias toward consistency in interpretation, action, and consequences. The problem is to find the correlating particulars by which to understand the nature of the moral idea, with integrity for what it implies for the social order and its future. The problem is to let freely evolve those influences that become eligible for resourceful development, while prohibiting those that destroy it.

The decisive cause of these connections between reason and nature, between ideas and facts, principles and practices, is the providential fact that people act on what they believe. They plant in the world, thereby, both their own adaptations to it and the contexts for understanding its meaning. Users and hearers of ideas—persons—are thus the third partner in this meaning triangle whereby the sense of an idea is transformed, every time that somebody acts reasonably, into an appropriate procedure. If the fittingness of these actions that may be said to reflect some basic moral law, such as freedom or justice, is violated by the false beliefs of irresponsible persons having no sense of history or no respect for consistency in social values, the guiding meaning of the moral idea may be forever lost. Then "freedom" may readily be made to signify "directed by the state." The great value of social memory and small-scale try-outs is that they bequeath to this process prudence and the watchful eye of experience.

The connection between ideas and facts moves in both directions. We can read the moral message off backwards: the many secondary norms, customs, and institutions that harmonize together, displaying a kind of family unity in repetition, can generate a transcendent moral ideal. That is to say, insight into related events and already developing social systems can induce a relevant and general idea. An eye to the originating precedents and their generic successors guides the meaning of this idea forward. Freedom not only means these empirical activities. It prevents their abuses. If these precedents and their ways of working are lost sight of, "the permanent things" (as T.S. Eliot called them) are lost sight of too. Their potential for actualization in living orders dies out from the center. What is left are empty phrases that no one knows how to fill. Now arise the dangerous moments when temptations and ignorance fix these remnant slogans coercively upon a people.

Solid and visible interactions that are seen to be humane and workable may be open-ended in history and nature but are not limitless in reason and logic. Reason and logic patrol their boundaries. "Thus," writes Burke,"...by preserving the method of nature in the conduct of the state, in what we improve we are never wholly new; in what we retain, we are never wholly obsolete." In time, certain specific practices take on the same eternal values as their guiding principle. Impartiality and neutrality in judgment, fair hearings on both sides, these concrete "determinations," these operational definitions or partial meaning postulates, have become logical derivatives of natural justice, so that we cannot imagine justice without them. They are essential to its fuller meaning. It is impossible to think of a just settlement without them. As we walk over the bridge into history, all the propitious details and fortifying provisions that we have come to know about and believe morally essential must remain fixed to the principle whose completeness comprehends and helps to identify the appropriate responses. Piecemeal practices are what we daily experience; but if we forget the deeper rhythm of the principle itself, we court a violent recasting in the law.

Vera Lex, Vol. 6, No. 1, 1986

GAUGING THE ESSENCE OF HEBREW LAW BY ITS CONSTRAINTS UPON POLITICAL POWER

Far be it from Thee to do such a thing, to slay the righteous with the wicked, so that the righteous and the wicked are treated alike. Far be it from Thee! Shall not the Judge of all the earth deal justly?
Genesis 18:25

Starting points, justifications, and even definitions of natural law have varied. But what has not varied is the practical function to which the natural law idea has been applied. This is the idea that the positive law, however authoritative its secular source, is answerable to a higher morality. Glenn Tinder has called it the "single indispensable idea in our past."[1] Laws and their administration, because they are coercive, are obligated to a code of morality (natural law), the violation of which destroys the character of the positive law and its legitimacy to compel. This overarching morality has the practical function, when legalized, of limiting and disciplining government; it furnishes a check on what those having political power may rightfully do. This

[1]Glenn Tinder, *Political Thinking, The Perennial Questions*. Boston: Little, Brown and Co., 1986. p. 32.

idea of a higher morality applied to the positive law dominates the jurisprudential natural law tradition.

The ethic of the Hebrew Scripture is a jurisprudential ethic. It is an ethic of just positive law. The traditional, customary, ritualistic and social relationships commanded and exemplified in the Hebrew Scripture are jurally and legislatively conceived. They are authoritative, and they furnish ground for enforceable judgment. Prophets warn and denounce. Priestly authority visits punitive sanctions on disobedience. Divine command severely rebukes, sometimes catastrophically punishes. The higher morality absorbed into the fundamental Hebrew positive law is judicial justice. "...to do justly, to love mercy, to walk humbly with our God."

According to Michel Villey, the political doctrines of Aristotle are also "defined in a perfectly firm and realistic way as the search for Justice [operating] firstly and principally by the observation of nature."[2] Hence this "original" natural law, Villey contends, is judicial.

Similarly, Stoic ethics, in stressing equality, the universal brotherhood of man, and the social order as a reflection of the spiritual order, carries obvious legal and juridical implications. These were emphatically realized by its Roman adopters.[3] "For law," said Cicero, out of the Stoic or philosophic natural law tradition, "is the bond of that dignity which we enjoy in the Republic. . . the foundation of liberty. . . the source of equity. . . . The magistrates who administer the law, the jurors who interpret the law—in fact all of us therefore—obey the law so that we may be free."

Accordingly, it appears that Aristotelian, Stoic (later Thomistic), and Hebrew law developed a parallel preoccupation with the just

[2] *Vera Lex*, Vol. VI, No. 1. Reprinted from the *Annual of Natural Law Study*, Vol. 2, 1968. Osaka, Japan.

[3] "...a medieval writer, seeking to expand the law of nature, had only to look about him to see actually operative in the world the Roman system which was the common heritage of every country, revered everywhere as the supreme triumph of human reason." J.L. Brierly, *The Law of Nations*. Reprinted in F.H. Lawson, Ed., *The Roman Law Reader*, Dobbs Ferry, N.Y.: Oceana Publications, Inc., 1969. P. 169.

community free from political usurpation and wrongdoing. It is in the interpersonal orders of just and unjust conduct, which includes the conduct of the ruler, that these ideas discover their practical application. In the Hebrew and Talmudic literature, prohibitions, requirements, duties and rights are at once morally construed and positively enforceable. The ethical positive law is both an obligation of the personal spirit in that special relation between God and men, and also an authoritative obligation with respect to those special relations between persons, especially because of the dangerous and evil nature of coercive power between the government and the governed. With respect to the actions of the Hebrew leaders, the positive law is continually corrected in the direction of a greater justice. The result of this restraint on coercive power that defines justice is, for the Hebrews (as with Cicero and the Stoic ideal of the natural law), freedom. It is the freedom to practice their faith that informs their communal experience. When the rule of law and corrections in the direction of a greater justice fail—when tyranny prevails—then civil disobedience, abolition, escape, or total revolt and the instituting of new government are justified as the moral solution, just as within the juridical tradition of natural law.

Abraham's departure from polytheistic Babylonia, the flight from Egypt under Moses, the Maccabean rebellion against the Hellenistic Syrians, the Zealots against the Romans—these events exemplify the moral right to define one's peoplehood in living under a law free from tyranny.

This idea from the Hebrew Testament went abroad and 1700 years later persisted in the minds of the American puritans escaping from oppression. Merchant, lawyer and Governor of the Massachusetts Bay Colony for 20 years, John Winthrop preached in his sermon to his fellow emigrants aboard the Arbella that took them to New England:

> Thus stands the cause between God and us. We are entered into covenant. . . to provide for our posterity, [and] to follow the counsel of Micah, to do justly, to love mercy, to walk humbly with our God . . . We must uphold a familiar commerce together,

> in all meekness, gentleness, patience, and liberality. We must delight in each other, make others' conditions our own, rejoice together, mourn together, labor and suffer together, always having before our eyes our commission and community. . . .[4]

Certain foundational ideas within Hebrew society correspond to seminal postures of the juridical natural law tradition. All have outstanding legal and judicial implications. The first foundational idea is God. When the Hebrews came to conceive the idea as universal, one God implied brotherhood, or moral equality. As a source of moral law, God stands transcendent over any positive law that man enforces; for coercion, unless vindicated by a moral norm of goodness, is evil. The giving of the law by this higher source, as with the Noahide laws or the Ten Commandments, suggests that some aspect of fundamental moral law is not of human origin; something of it supersedes human desire and approval, even agreement. Here God's nature, in being both authoritative and good, awakens man's own capacity for reasoned judgment. Man's judgment is not fully autonomous; but in being rational it can understand the higher moral law as being in conformity with what God's goodness authorizes. God would not put human nature under an irrational moral command.

A second foundational idea is Covenant. A mutual promise entails the willing participation and commitment of those who promise. When God is party to a promise, the contract may be enduring. Certainly the benefits are hardly questionable. In the idea of a contract and a promise, and in the philosophical use to which the "social contract" has been put, the Hebraic Covenant has had a lasting continuity in the tradition of natural law as an instrument against political domination. A third idea is the Rule of Law. Rule structured law is general and equal in scope and application. Hence in excluding exception, it excludes privilege in the will of the sovereign.

[4] "A Model of Christian Charity," 1630. Reprinted in Samuel Eliot Morison, Ed., *Old South Leaflets*, No. 207. Old South Association, Boston, MA.

These broad, morally authoritative ideas set the framework for the principles and practices that define the day-by-day legal maintenance of the Hebrew community. What are these principles and practices? Equality of persons before the law, establishment of independent courts of justice, sanctity of promise, responsibility, rights of persons and groups, the right to criticize government, local self-rule, and importantly, respect for the human dignity of persons the deepest moral and religious foundation of law. "The injunction upon each Israelite to deal justly with his fellows thereby became more than the defense of rights of property or persons; it became a defense of human dignity."[5]

Concrete events, too, in the biblical experience exemplify these ethical-legal principles and practices and the constraint on government they imply. Moses was chastised by God for his arrogance and was forbidden, even after his courageous government, to enter the Promised Land. He was never made king. Thus not to be privileged, Moses too was brought under the rule of law. Gideon was made judge and asked by the Israelites to rule over them. "I will not rule over you," Gideon replied, "neither shall my son rule over you; the Lord shall rule over you." Samuel warned the people not to establish a kingship lest they, too, "like all the nations," become victims of despotism.

> "Give us a king to judge us. . ."And [Samuel] said, This will be the manner of the king that shall reign over you: He will take your sons and appoint them for himself, for his chariots, and to be his horsemen. . .and to make his instruments of war. . .and he will take your fields, and your vineyards and your olive yards, even the best of them, and give them to his servants. And he will take the tenth of your seed and of your vineyards, and give it to his officers and to his servants.

[5] Orlinsky, Harry M. *Ancient Israel* (2nd ed.), Ithaca, N.Y.: Cornell University Press, 1963. I am indebted to the profound insights into Hebrew thought contained in Orlinsky's book.

> Nevertheless, the people refused to obey the voice of Samuel...[6]

However magnificent in other ways, the kings of the United Kingdom of Israel exceeded their powers. They centralized the administration; forced labor without compensation; levied oppressive taxes; redistricted tribal boundaries so as to weaken tribal power and independence. Despotism in kingship did not have to wait a thousand years for Herod to appear! These corruptions did not escape without punishment. When the higher morality that defined the rule of law was transgressed, vindictive lessons resulted. Saul, the first king, was not impeached for his haughty disregard of the law and usurpation of the priestly offices; but Saul went mad, and his beloved son Jonathan was killed in battle. David was not impeached for complicity in murderous actions against Uriah or for putting up his military might against his faith; but he was denounced by the prophet Nathan, pestilence visited seventy thousand of his men, and his beloved son Absalom deceived and revolted against him. Solomon was not impeached for pagan polygamy and idolatry, or for his failure to keep the judgments and statutes of the kingdom; but just retribution fell upon him by adversaries and the kingship was taken away from the Davidic dynasty he inherited. "Behold I will rend the kingdom out of the hand of Solomon."

Poignantly, confusion and conflict, reversal and retribution threw this judicial morality into the foreground, teaching what is lawfully right by the way of what is morally wrong. What is the message? The meaning and experience of juridical justice and the rule of law that are the practical provenance of natural law's enduring past, are omnipresent in the Hebraic scriptural literature. They begin at the beginning with Abraham's appeal to the Lord, "Shall not the Judge of all the earth deal justly?" and they continue to the end.

Virginia Black—Vera Lex, Vol. VI, No. 2, 1986

[6] Samuel 8: 11-19.

WHAT KINDS OF LAW NEED CHANGING?

Those who seek to legislate new laws which require a departure from established law, often seek change in accord with what the jurist Oliver Wendell Holmes (USA) called "the felt necessities of the times." They think such changes bring law up to date. But to bring law up to date demands a corresponding account of a new place and a new time. So we hear such justifications for new law as "law that is special to today's market," "law's place in the new world," "what the law will become in the first half of the 21st century," and even reference to constitutional provisions that are "out of date," and so presumably must be modernized. (When the constitutional provisions that are referred to have provided fitting adjustments for several hundred years, one wonders what "up to date" could imply.)

It is true that much of the positive law is particularistic with respect to time and place. It often must be brought "up to date" when its purpose is to meet unexpected developments. Certainly catastrophic events require quick and apt legal accommodation. Society undergoes internal changes not by evenly measured units but unpredictably, even chaotically at times. Hence the law that is adjusted to novelties, or is interpreted on behalf of deliberate management of situations—administrative law—is rightly temporary when what it needs to regulate are circumstances that are different because they are truly new or details that implement a timely and proper purpose of governance. And of course, such law means much law.

The error is to take "the felt necessities of the times" to mean that all times exhibit new felt necessities and in all manners and respects, so that in order to accommodate wholistic change, all law is replaceable. Hence, allegedly, the constitution, too, the foundational law that belongs to moral society as its outgrowth, must continually be replaced by decisionary fiat to meet new and different times. A position like this one that addresses all law at once—the foundation with the frame—describes legal and moral relativism since in abandoning universal right as part of itself, it excludes the moral substrata of natural society. It is these moral substrata of natural society that proper constitutions define.

Relativism in law is appropriate only with specific relationships in unrecurring situations, and positivism only where efficiencies and not evils prevail. They are not appropriate for the social order as a whole at levels where serious moral thought defines the permanent importance of norms of just social cohesion, forbidding their violation. Old law may be "old" only because being abiding, it was discovered early and has perseverated. It may have perseverated because being abiding, it is also continually new.

A false assumption lies behind the repetitious call for new law at all levels indiscriminately. It makes no distinction between the edicts-of-the-times-and-the-place and the law of social cohesion among free individuals which we call the Constitution, a term for preserving under the highest law what society is constituted of. This is like making no distinction between the pious rituals of an historical moment and lasting things of the spirit which are shared in common. The false assumption is that old law is relative only to its own outmoded time and place. Since new needs and desires have arisen and since new technology has determined new values and new culture, new complex societies require new, complex laws. "Everything is changing so fast that nothing at all is what it used to be."

The belief that every law is relative only to its own history and therefore that one's own law must be relative only to currencies, overlooks the fact that some social conditions, old and new, then and now, forever do not change. The common denominators of social order as such are always the same. The law should parallel and respect them.

Those who seek to legislate new laws as a departure from established law on behalf of "the felt necessities of the times," confuse not new with old, but types of law. They confuse not what is earlier and later but what is temporary with what is lasting. They confuse general with administrative law, equal and abiding law with the coercive directives sometimes needed to get things done, or politically to govern.

In tribal societies, for example, survival and security are perceived to depend upon common efforts toward common goals; and there seems to prevail a mysterious superstition that people have to be directed by authority to get things done. Accordingly, politics are centralized with an eye to the concrete details that complete a common project. Control over results so as to mandate redirection quickly and to effect the end in accordance with the vision—digging a well, building a pyramid, distributing food, securing a territory—demands coercion of the specifics of person and circumstance. In free societies, general and equal law lets individuals choose their course and chart their ends. In tribal societies, details are managed from the center, dictated by officials enforcing this mandate here or there, that edict now or then. Preoccupied with their own "felt necessities of the times," tribal societies are statist societies. Collective awareness drowns the individual like tidal waves sinking ships at sea.

Such legal relativism, "law" relative not just to the place or time but to each situation as defined by the supreme authorities, and its cohort, legal positivism, describe the oldest form of government we know; it is the most dominant political structure history has revealed to us. But this is not law. It is oppression. Those who wish law always brought up to date are opting, in their ignorance, not for moral and legal advance but for the mores of the tribe with its administrative authority that locks out personal freedom.

Tribal societies exist today, for they are a perpetual type of no particular size, not an antiquity. Their ideology requires relativism and so, positivism. All their decrees are subject to change and dissolution by the whim of politics. Such states are not new and modern, up to date or "in keeping with the times." Their type is as old as ancient Babylon and the Kingdom of Akkad. Quite clearly it is not a matter of old and new at all. It is a matter of preserving—or of failing to preserve—the fundamentals of law that allow society to order itself by respecting the worth of the citizen in deciding his own actions on the basis of the particulars that only he knows and can evaluate regarding how he wants to forward or maintain his situation. When this foundational order of natural society and its basic or constitutive law are submerged by administrative fiats rationalized as adjustments to new complexities ("the felt necessities of the times"), the result is the tribe, a political type that morally advancing civilization should have left behind.

In fact, complexities in the social phalanx require simplicities and leanness at the center to allow full play in the ranks, and adjustments at the edges which only free persons can effectively devise. These simplicities are none other than general and equal law. They are Constitutional law. So long as the propensities of human social nature remain the same, such law changes neither its content nor its contour. Difficult, impermanent features of life require the almost forgotten verities to negotiate their resolution, especially through difficult, impermanent times like ours. And, indeed, if we keep it clear, change, from the obscuring myth of what is universal and abiding may even be found in every concrete situation.

It is paradoxic in our age of awareness of One World that that which is relative and not universal should enjoy so many popularizers. It is paradoxic that despite the universalistic spirit of our times in which we speak not only of natural but of human rights, the relativism that implies positivism should spawn the claim that "the constitution is out of date." Today's One World spirit reflects an outlook on mankind as a whole that can only be called universal. This means that certain principles, those that preserve just society and respect for morally equal persons, are always appropriately invoked even when they cannot immediately be made effective. They caution against intolerance of the diverse networks of peaceable, associative relations that bind free peoples to each other. These principles and the legal postulates that protect them are not to be manipulated by claims that "new times" demand a departure from "old law," without first demonstrating that there is nothing permanent in the old law that is adequate for human good. In facing the challenge of that which is true and good for us now, we face the greater challenge of discerning that which is true and good for us always.

Vera Lex, Vol. VII, No. 2, 1987

THE TEXT: ITS SOURCES AND SIGNIFICANCE FOR MANKIND

It is important to insist that there is a text. But what does this mean? It means, for our purposes, that a moral principle is set forth or a moral judgment is made which is intended to direct or to criticize someone acting in a specifiable way. That principle or that moral judgment is what I call a text. The natural law is such a text. The text, we might say, is the full meaning of the natural law, both in its abstract and concrete fulfillments.

The text which we call the natural law is not without ambiguity and vagueness, historical variations and subjective differences. And it is never complete—it is brazen to believe we have discovered all the moral truth that exists. But by and large, the natural law, though incomplete, is a recognizable set of moral principles. Since their contradiction, denial, distortion or violation are recognizable as well, this implies that their meaning, though indefinite, nevertheless has boundaries: There are limits to how the natural law as a set of moral principles can be validly interpreted and applied. It is false, as we say, that "anything goes." Not all judgments and actions are morally acceptable. There is, as we say, a text.

Why should we require a text? We require a text so that we can guide, and if necessary constrain, what people do to one another. By and large, humankind prefers social stability to conflict and chaos. Humankind prefers moral knowledge to moral nihilism; security and predictability to uncertainty; freedom to coercion. But there is something in us that also inclines us to partisanship, and so we often prefer our own interests and those of our group to those of the common good of the community or of the nation or the world. This partisan tendency predisposes us to some degree of moral blindness.

Partisanship, moreover, inclines us to force others to do what is good not for them but for ourselves.

In binding the range of interpretation of generally understood and agreed-to moral ways of interacting, our partisan inclinations are checked and curbed. As a result, a larger dose of good will and social stability and a lesser amount of social chaos are brought about. And our personal freedom is given a broader range of opportunity.

Two tendencies have unfortunately characterized the history and experience of mankind. They destroy the text. They blur and ridicule the discipline of limited, responsible interpretation. One is the tendency to elevate moral principles too high, to build utopias, idealized visions, "Committees of Virtue," heavenly cities—and impose them on mankind. By this tendency, human nature is forgotten. The other tendency goes to the opposite extreme. It reduces moral goodness and moral obligation to self-interest, to raw want, will, impulse and power. It lowers the "ought" to the "is." It cynically denies the capacity of persons to act without ulterior motives, to act without partisanship, to act hospitably with fellow feeling and to forward the community good. It too forgets human nature.

We can avoid these twin false tendencies that lead into nihilism on the one hand, coercion on the other. We can cling closely to the text. This requires us to deny that "anything goes." To deny that moral imperatives can be interpreted in any way whatsoever. To deny that meaning is corruptible, words can be played with, rules can be reduced and arbitrarily applied, anybody's subjective will or want is correct, any community's preferred ways are right, any text can be "deconstructed."

Deconstruction is the newest academic fad. Deconstruction is a technique of analysis that denies stable meaning to a text. Devaluing the authority of the text shifts interpretation to the will of the commentator. No range of interpretation ever is determinate. No constraints on meaning ever win legitimacy. Deconstruction should be called destructivism. Not only does it reduce a text to sets of meaningless statements by its assumption of value-nihilism and its denial of the objectivity of perceptions and propositions. These latter also become subject to any claim that some one wants to make. Deconstruction reduces to power the legitimacy of moral authority. From the perspective of deconstruction, morality is how those in power persuade those who are not in power to submit to their view, even their coercion. Hence with respect to laws, policies, and legal decisions, deconstruction means: The powerful win.

Those who search for an authentic text, as I do, think that the full meaning of a moral principle and its operative judgments lies somewhere in between the extremes of a utopian element in moral meaning and its deconstructive replacement by egotistic wants. The text despises flights of fancy just as it despises their replacement by the reductionist's claim that brute reality cannot be changed by moral conduct or that moral conduct is self-aggrandizement in disguise.

One way to cling to the text is to cling to human experience and to a view of man as exhibited by history and its realistic perspectives and visions. Clinging to the text is being informed of the context within which a moral imperative originates and knowing what interpretations have already been given it and which of them has worked in the past to affect a desired end. Human experience and history demonstrate that persons are capable of fairness and hospitality, beneficence and selfless obligations; self-serving is not the full history of the common man. But human experience and history also demonstrates that self-interest normally prevails and so the heavenly city of brotherhood and equity cannot prevail on earth.

The larger perspectives of history and experience and the special insights brought to us by those who are thought to be wise can aid individuals who are seeking moral understanding for their actions in escaping the solipsism of their errors. They can also aid those who criticize the moral judgments of others. Moral agents and moral critics should refer to the larger picture of history and experience which contain within their frame the limits of the text.

Without a fixed referent, the text—what we believe we morally owe each other—turns into promiscuous dreams from which no prudent dialogue, decision, or reform whatsoever can ensue. But also without an image of something better than what exists at the moment, no motivation, zeal or discipline to persist can carry the present into the future. What is essential, therefore, is to preserve and to cherish the text. The natural law is a named text that embodies for human use the reasonable and efficable requirements of the moral life.

Vera Lex, Vol. IX, No. 1, 1989

LEGAL EQUITY AND ITS MISUSE

. . .discretion is not necessarily lawless. When we praise showing fine discretion on any occasion, we certainly do not mean that he has acted in an anarchic manner. Discretion, in general, represents more or less instinctive evaluation or appreciation of the diverse elements that enter into a complex; and such instinctive evaluation must precede conscious rule making.

—Morris Cohen, *Law and the Social Order*

In the 17th century, Queen Elizabeth I of England had a holiday with equity, that dimension of justice that looks more closely at the situation, at the individual case and, as they say in medicine, takes not only the disease into account but the host into account. Elizabeth found equity a convenient tool for the power politics she required to overstep an independent judiciary. She needed to make a claim that looked morally legitimate under the valid rubric, "state's interest," but she intended this claim at the same time to advance her power. Observing that the Court of Chancery in England functioned (and rightfully) outside legal rules of action (which were kept jealously within their judicial, historic provenance, their meanings bound by the exclusive and independent guilds of courts of law), Elizabeth was clever enough to know that dispensing with rules and precedent opens the gate for discretion. Discretion can wobble in unpredictable directions. This is what she wanted of it. Using the English equity court, Star Chamber, to rid herself of personal threats to her throne, "equity" became "state's interest"—*as defined by herself and her cohorts!*

Not exactly the intended function of an equity decision as an integral part of justice. Equity is a paradoxical idea. Law is rules, and equity defies application of rules. It necessarily does this whenever their application fails to do justice to the case at hand since rules of law are only, anyway, a means to the higher end of justice. We could not understand equity without this higher end. And so equity looks not at like cases (which rules nicely accommodate) but at differences, at what is peculiar or extraordinary about a situation. Equity looks at uniqueness in the individual situation. And to do this well, it has to employ discretion on the part of the judge. Hopefully his discretion is intelligent and virtuous. Hopefully his conscience is clean. Hopefully, his values are upright.

The explicit introduction of equity into Western moral and legal, though, treasonably follows Aristotle's formulation in Book V of the *Nicomachean Ethics* (and later in *Rhetoric*) in which equity is seen as a different sort of justice:

> there are some cases about which it is not possible to pronounce a general statement correctly; and so. . .there are matters on which it is impossible to lay down a law. What is itself indeterminate must also have an indeterminate rule.

Yet allied as equity has rightly been with natural law as the moral component of the positive law, its history has not shown continuous integrity in application. This is because the idea of equity is, in itself, so amorphous that rationalized justifications can slip by the careless or self-empowering jurist. Certainly this is unfortunate. But how can we ever do justice without the principles and standards of equity that, in the absence of relevant law, help to guide and to limit the necessary discretion?

No one shall profit from his own evil doing. One may not induce another to act to his detriment. Give to each that which is his due. Equity soothes injury. Nulla poena sine leges. Judgment must be made in light of what the reasonable person would likely do. The accused must be confronted with his crime. Such are the principles of equity.

Current in America is a legal case in which a burglar trying to gain entry into someone's house fell through a skylight. He sued and recovered $26,000 for his injuries! Equity is made a fool. And justice is depraved by such a decision. Equity soothes injury. Whose injury? Under what circumstances? Equity also forbids evil to profit.

There is no doubt that equity has been misapplied. And indeed, raw, barebone equity shorn of its traditional and intended uses, shorn of context, purpose, precedent and responsible interpretation, invites such misapplication. Through the substitution of mindless and self-serving decisions for the reasoned opinions of an impersonal, fair-minded conscience, equity has served immoral masters—or, often, moral masters in an unintelligent mood. The amorphous nature of equity requires that it be held within the limits of official precedent, institutional practice, and the related moral and legal principles that bind its operation.

Now clearly equity is and has been an appropriate natural law intervention into the positive law of statute and rule-based judgment. Equity is the rationally moral part of curial judgment whatever doing justice necessitates applied to the higher standards idea of a relevant difference. In this respect, lacking the clear limitations of rule-guidance, the essential orientation of equity is *attention to details*—the differentiating facts of the case which in their conglomerate seem to be unique—and its application is to the individual partly who without equity would allegedly be wronged. "Treat like cases alike" does not here at all pertain. Similarities pertain to equalities only when things relevantly are the same. But it is differences that count with equitability. Stealing is forbidden by law. But for a hungry man to steal bread to feed his children, it is equitable "to consider a man's intention and not his act" (Aristotle, *Rhetoric*). How foolish it would be to drive forward into a busy intersection on the green light (which lawfully I am in the right to do) while an intricate construction operation at the intersection clearly shows me it is dangerous to proceed. Unremitting application of the law is often stupid. "What the reasonable person would do," an important standard of equity, conflicts with the law in many cases. Thus does legal equity require the genius of a *local and personal adjustment to fit new or extraordinary situations.*

Today, once again, equity has, it seems, been misapplied. In the modern nation, equity has become a vast, administrative sovereign. It has become an abject slave of "public policy." Equity is loyalty to intent, displaying justice through respect for the personal circumstance, the situated differences of the case. But today, equity has been interpreted to mean, instead of an equitable allocation through the particular and unique, an equal allocation through the same and the general. If I do not like chocolate cake, it is inequitable to serve me up a piece just because everyone is getting a piece of chocolate cake. A chocolate cake divided equally is not equitable if those to whom it is served are not equal, not the same, in their needs or tastes or situations. We violate equity when we act in the same way, or provide equal products and provender, to people unequal in their circumstances. No one is ever equal—everyone is different in their circumstances. We do not want our difference, when relevant to a distinction, to make no difference a fixed referent to what is distributed.

"Equality is equity" goes the maxim. Only when cases which look alike are alike, a distinction not easily made from a distance. Before the rule of thumb, "treat like cases alike" can be implemented, it is first necessary to examine cases at close range to discern whether they are indeed alike, or only appear so. Nor does the doling out of lookalike goods by political agencies create like cases.

The vast, modern, administrative state in the name of equity has taken on, these days, the dispensation of equality. From the center, far from the visibility which the local perspective provides, it dispenses goods that are the same. But it dispenses these goods to persons whose conditions and needs are intricately different from one another. And it dispenses from the center what can only effectively be adjudicated and adjusted at the periphery. In the name of being equitable, it ignores that equitability has always meant treating lookalikes but actually different cases differently. The vast, modern, administrative state is not capable of treating such cases differently. And so it translates equity into equal; for it is far easier and efficient to dispense things that look alike to people that, from a distance, also look alike than with painstaking patience to respect the adaptation essential to individual settlements recognized for their merits and differences.

Do I sense that a fallacy is committed here? Judicial equity is discretionary. Administration is also discretionary. Therefore the role of public administration is equity (that is, an equal distribution of the product).

Is it redundant to remark once again that when the centralized state gets into the act of what requires moral discrimination, or equity, it necessarily fails? That is to say, the intended effect is not the actual effect. The actual effect is to enhance the powers of those in government.

Under the high principle of natural justice, has equity once again become the "state's interest"? Has Queen Elizabeth I of England been reincarnated to deceive us under another, this time more subtle disguise?

Vera Lex, Vol. XI, No. 1, 1991

WHY WE MUST REFER TO A NATURAL LAW

(A contribution to the continuing column, "The Controversy Up to Date: A critical examination of the resources of natural law in answer to the charges of its critics.")

Vagueness in the natural law leads to a parallel vagueness of natural in the practical applications laws—so goes a familiar charge. An abstract natural law gives no guidance to statutes, policies, legal judgments and judicial decisions, not to speak of moral judgments and decisions. Critics therefore assert that natural laws and their alleged vague referents may be eliminated without loss. Natural laws, they claim, count for nothing because they do not work; they are inoperative. They provide no control over the specific contents of moral and juridical judgment, and do little service, as well, for situated moral decisions where concrete circumstances have to lead the way.

Wanton killing or assaulting of persons, committing personal injury, damaging people's property, using others for ulterior, malevolent gain—even these interdictions may still be so broadly general as not effectively to guide precision of judgment. But because these well-known, intermediately vague rules of wrongdoing may somewhat guide judgment, help us to assemble relevant facts or reach relevant conclusions, it is superfluous, to invoke, it is argued, a "natural law." It seems adequate to invoke directly these more specific prohibitions and define their participating classes of action. That such prohibitions may also be natural laws is as idle to mention, goes the argument, as that our more serious legal prohibitions often parallel and reflect our more serious moral prohibitions. Since everyone knows this already, must we say of every criminal act, ". . . and oh! by the way, it is also a moral evil," or, "What you have done is a violation of natural law!"

But surely one has to ask: If intermediately vague laws can guide legal judgment, as they do, where exactly is the fine, discriminating line between what is too vague and what is not?

The above charges against natural law are all quite true insofar as they speak to a rhetorical redundancy. But I think they are trivial and of little account. For overriding the objection that summoning reference to natural law is often unnecessary and admits into the discourse vagueness when we already have intermediate injunctions to work with, I believe there are pragmatic vindications of natural law that are arrestingly useful and significant.

Reference to natural law in legal and judicial contexts is significant and useful because such a reference serves to refer, remind, retort, and remember. And it may also, by forcing the mind to a higher-level purpose, change the results.

1. After driving on the same wheels for a time, law and its serpentine reasoning look terribly artificial, hard to understand, technical and trivial. Here is where the citizen loses his way, sensing within himself confusion, resentment and anger building against the profession. These dysfunctional emotions occur in us within a social matrix that is already today too confusing and complex to deal with without despair. When the citizen yearns to remake the route he thinks he should be traveling, he yearns for a purpose he can understand and empathize with. Natural law principles ring an immediate and familiar bell in the instinctual inclinations of civilized peoples. Knowing that these principles guide the law is a soothing relief from the distempers of our modern despair.

2. When reference to natural law repeats something that is already known, making this reference explicit reminds us that moral checks are often needed on the positive law, putting to the chase the ever-recurring fear of tyranny. Chains of reasoning within the positive law are insufficient for this vital truth that laid, for example, the foundation of the American political heritage. If they were sufficient, the Americans would never have needed to reformulate and make explicit the "ancient liberties" they believed were disregarded by the British Parliament and Crown. These "ancient liberties" were written as fundamental rights—and what, by comparison with the written findings of the common law, could be more vague?

3. Vagueness in laws such as rights expands the idea so that unforeseen situations—the future—can be brought within the ambit of the present. Because vagueness is part of the rational it is comprehensive procedure for sorting out resembling cases.

The material order and whatever is good about it cannot long survive without its correlate in immaterial fixed stars. Certainly it cannot become the best that lies within its potential.

4. Natural law reminds us of a domain of reason, ideality, and principled, ethical imagination that transcends the vote, the poll, the consensus, the treaty, and the norm. These are transitory tools. Serious moral weight binds in a way that legal decisions as authoritative, convenient, or mandated by "the necessities of the times" can never bind. The morality of law cannot be taken for granted, nor, in its turn, can moral obligations be automatically registered as laws. Nevertheless, something intrinsic to what is enforced best describes what cannot be morally tolerated. Humanly constructed contingencies are subject to manipulation and neglect, sometimes to ridicule and covert dismissal. If we want legal solutions to legal problems and not a discretionary stretching of some judge's current conscience, these can be secured only when certain fundamental morals live within the law. Such a marriage can often make a compelling and substantive difference in moral and legal results. How that extraordinarily vague concept "due process" has worked over the years to shape the positive law toward justice is a paradigmatic example.

5. When natural law provides even only a reminder that in the positive law not anything goes, then natural law performs a beneficial function for our human psyche, our conscience, our motivation, and for our extraordinarily desperate times.

A reminder even of general principle, howsoever vague—"No harm is to be done," "Fair treatment demands equal consideration," "Live justly," "Persons are of equal dignity," "The worst should be subordinate to the better"—is essential to discovering legal applications consonant with a civic order in which humanity's moral development is foremost. From empty formalism any restive movement that any majority, faction, bench, or sovereignty endorses can become the law. In critical times, the foolish belief that we can ignore fundamental things with impunity is a treacherous plight to ponder. And if there is such a thing as a sense of right, verbal references to "good" and "equal," however vague, can give us pause to remember.

6. Situations arise when we need to ask ourselves once again why this or that law was, or should be, instituted. Answers to these questions need to reach beyond the immediate purpose that our laws are meant to satisfy, beyond the mischief that our laws are meant to repel. What are we to answer to this deeper quest? The assembly decreed it? People want it? Precedent requires it? Legislative compromise demands it? How unsatisfying to the mind is this bald reference to political power, even that power which hides behind the law. How, when we discover its ruses, such a blank, reason-stopping impasse incites us to resentment and rebellion! Comprehending, on the other hand, that the positive law maintains an ineluctable moral ground and comprehending something of what this moral ground has meant in its historical renditions acknowledges our motivation and satisfies our reason.

7. A further practical advantage in vitalizing the positive law with natural law is this: a positive law becomes necessary whenever lack of enforcement weakens persons' reciprocal inclinations to do that which is morally obligatory. Hence the positive law has to demonstrate an enduring character if we are reliably to call on it to validate what we believe is ethically necessary to express what is universal in our human nature. Without such vindication, ordering the community through the instruments of a stable and reasonable justice is an impossible task. Today's peoples are unsettled and migrant. It seems likely that we shall soon and permanently be living among each other. Considering its meaning and its consequences, are we to endure, then, another Tower of Babel? Not to believe that despite their differences, the peoples of the globe have something in common that can be reinforced by the positive law is to allow our fears to destroy us. It is to live forgetting tomorrow.

To come to terms with this necessity, compelling in our times, some laws have to be steadfast, expectable, intransigent, and universal in spirit. What can be more trustworthy than lining one's civic constitution with firm principles of social interaction that cannot be repealed or made void by the next election or hate campaign? To allege that this higher law is dispensable is to allow that every law can be here today and gone tomorrow, pandering to the transitory interest of exclusionist prejudices, and hence totally unprepared for propitious change. With nothing enduring to ground it—with law's content, forms, applications, dissoluble and practices at will—the gate is open to social fear and apocalyptic turmoil.

Laws unanchored and autonomous tend to corrupt, in time, human integrity in matters of allegiance and reciprocity, public matrices that law has principally evolved to secure. A primary function of the positive law is fixing itself with such relative stability on the social landscape as to enable persons to know, plan, anticipate, and craft the social institutions they always need: the stabilizing intermediaries between individuals and their communitarian visions. Without natural law as a comprehensive telos working toward ends always superior than the present, the positive law is blind; it is a means only . . . . to what?

Vera Lex, Vol. XII, No. 2, 1992

CONTRIBUTORS

Virginia Black is editor emeritus of *Vera Lex* and Professor emeritus of Philosophy at Pace University, Pleasantville, New York.

William Pencak is Professor of American History at Pennsylvania State University. In addition to two books on Massachusetts history and two edited books on New York history, his recent work includes *Jews and Gentiles in Early America* (University of Michigan Press, 2005).

David Lorenzo Izquierdo is Assistant Professor of Ethics and Political Philosophy at Universidad Internacional de Cataluna (Barcelona, Spain). His most recent work is *Comunitarismo contra individalismo: una revision de los valores de Occidente desde el pensamiento de A. MacIntyre* (Thomas-Aranzadi, Madrid, 2007).

William C. Plouffe, Jr., J.D. is Assistant Professor of Criminal Justice at Kutztown University of Pennsylvania. Among his publications are "Sovereignty in the New World Order," *Tulsa Journal of Comparative and International Law,* vol. 7 (2000); "Mongolian Bankruptcy Law: A Comparative Analysis with the American Bankruptcy System," *Tulsa Journal of Comparative and International Law*, vol. 4.1 (1999).

Paul Cornish is Director of the Centre for Defense Studies, King's College London. He has served in the British Army and the Foreign and Commonwealth Office and at the Royal Institute of International Affairs (Chatham House). He has lectured in the Defense Studies Department of King's College London (Joint Services Command and Staff College) and at the University of Cambridge and was NATO Research Fellow 2000-2002. Among his recent publications are "The Ethics of 'effect-based' warfare: the crowding out of jus in bello" in *The Price of Peace: Just War Theory in the Twenty-first Century*, eds. Charles Reed & David Ryall (Cambridge University Press, 2007); *The Conflict in Iraq*, 2003, ed. Paul Cornish (Palgrave MacMillan, 2004). He is currently Assistant Professor of Political Science, Grand Valley State University.

A small number of back copies of VERA LEX remain at a cost of USD $10.00 a copy.* A complete back set of VERA LEX is $115.00 (see list below). Those who order will receive, without charge, all five previous graphically reproduced issues neatly bound: Vol. 1, No. 1 (1979) through Vol. III, No. 1 (1982). [Vol. II No. 2 was not issued.] For more information on Pace titles, please visit the website: http://www.pace.edu/press

1982 Vol. III,	No. 2	**Reason in the Natural Law**
1986 Vol. VI,	No. 1	**Edmund Burke and the Natural Law: Theory and Practice**
	No. 2	**Is There a Natural Law in Hebrew Tradition?**
1987 Vol. VII,	No. 1	**Natural Law and Constitutionalism**
	No. 2	**Natural Law and Constitutionalism II**
1988 Vol. VIII,	No. 1	**Rights I**
	No. 2	**Rights II**
1989 Vol. IX,	No. 1	**(General Interest)**
	No. 2	**The Spanish Tradition** (Index: Yves R. Simon)
1990 Vol. X,	No. 1	**Thomas Aquinas**
	No. 2	**(General Interest)**
1991 Vol. XI,	No. 1	**Equity as Natural Law**
	No. 2	**Sacred and Secular Natural Law**
1992 Vol. XII,	No. 1	**Jurisprudence and the Natural Law**
	No. 2	**Legal Positivism, Pragmatism**
1993 Vol. XIII, Nos. 1&2 (double issue) (Rosmini, Trigeaud)		**Dignity as Natural Law**
1994 Vol. XIV, Nos. 1&2 (double issue)		**Empirical Natural Law, Human Nature, Science**
1995 Vol. XV, Nos. 1&2 (double issue) (Includes 6-year cumulative index: 1990–1995)		**Autonomy, Independence, Liberty**

2000 New Series Vol. I Nos. 1&2 (double issue)	**Natural Law and Natural Environment** (available direct from Pace UP)
2001 New Series Vol. II Nos. 1&2 (double issue)	**Liberalism and Natural Law** (available direct from Pace UP)
2002 New Series Vol. III Nos. 1&2 (double issue)	**Globalism and Natural Law** (available direct from Pace UP)
2003 New Series Vol. IV Nos. 1&2 (double issue)	**Feminism and Natural Law** (available direct from Pace UP)
2004 New Series Vol. V Nos. 1&2 (double issue)	**Medieval Natural Law Theories** (available direct from Pace UP)
2005 New Series Vol. VI Nos. 1&2 (double issue)	**The Work of John Finnis** (available direct from Pace UP)
2006 New Series Vol. VII Nos. 1&2 (double issue)	**Natural Law Theory & Asian Thought** (available direct from Pace UP)
2007 New Series Vol. VIII Nos. 1&2 (double issue)	**(General Interest)** (available direct from Pace UP)

***Two back issues of VERA LEX are out of print. However, the originals are available in xeroxed form for USD $5.00.**

1983–84 Vol. IV, Nos. 1&2 (double issue)	**Hugo Grotius** (index)
1985 Vol. V No. 1 (No. 2 was not issued.)	**Giambattista Vico**

Official Journal of the International Association for Environmental Philosophy

Environmental Philosophy

$40 ($25 for students) annually with membership to International Association for Environmental Philosophy

$25 individual non-membership subscription

Send payment to:
Kenneth Maly
Department of Philosophy
University of Wisconsin-LaCrosse,
LaCrosse, WI 54601

Published by the International Association for Environmental Philosophy, the University of Wisconsin-LaCrosse and the Division of the Environment, University of Toronto

www.ingramcontent.com/pod-product-compliance
Lightning Source LLC
LaVergne TN
LVHW022047200926
848481LV00003B/812
* 9 7 8 0 9 4 4 4 7 3 9 2 4 *